Epistolary Rex

Peter Case
&
David Ensminger

Dedicated to the memories of friends

Tim O'Brien, writer/activist,

Scott Wannberg, poet

and

Kathy Johnston, musician

"How dull (and copyclerkish) it would be to write at one's best all the time. How idle to praise freedoms, and do your own work like a slave."

-- Kenneth Patchen, 1946

Front cover photograph by David Ensminger

Back cover photograph by Trish Herrera

Cover design by J.R. Delgado

LOTD PRESS
leftofthedialmag@hotmail.com

(Peter Case)

How do you explain to someone what a musician is? A poet? Everybody makes everything today, and that's good, but what about real magic? What about knowledge and authority?

What about luck?

Sittin' here at the kitch table, Miles' Bitches Brew blasting out of the stereo in the front room, it's July 7, 2011, hot, got the doors open for air, hope the nabes are diggin' these far out sounds on the street, right now Chick Corea is 'soloing,' funky bluesy plus complete chaos of attack and release, the whole band layin' in thick behind him, New Orleans plus Hendrix, Dylan's bass player, that's Harvey Brooks, then... quiet, and now here's Miles again, and goin' back up the ladder, it's musical madness, a harrowing 3-d picture of New York street life, pretty accurate, ha, I was there around that time, and I dug the hell out of Miles then too, when I was 15. I didn't have to grow up to dig it. But as I grew up I could keep diggin' it more... and that's my question: what happened to KNOWLEDGE? The inside beam on street culture?

People laugh at 'poetry', scoff at 'jazz', think they know 'history,' while 'science' and 'violence' rule. But do they really?

Wayne Shorter and Miles are playing the melody now to 'Sanctuary' in unison, first as a ballad, then the band explodes: the sound of the city, torn up, heartbroken, hidden. The music is not goal oriented, Miles knows there's 'nowhere to run' and nothing to be grabbed in a hurry, just the hang, the musical clock, electric meditational voodoo, endless days of kids on corners... trouble, and love, too. It's all here.

Wayne and Miles and Herbie (Hancock) too had already been together for years. They had an understanding, a system, even if they changed up 180 on the acoustics. And Miles was the father, the leader, the frontman, the singular voice, and nobody in the world knew what he knew, or could sound like him.

It's called authority.

Ginsberg had it. Dylan. Jerry Garcia. Aretha Franklin. Otis and Jimi.

Henry Rollins? Joe Strummer?

Sonic Youth while we're at it? Thurston Moore and Lee Renaldo? It's a sense of coming from somewhere bearing KNOWLEDGE... fascinating secret inside juice.

And that's what we're livin' for!

Poets and musicians and painters. Filmmakers. Athletes... Jim Brown flickin' off the ball like a POS after a touchdown run. Joe Namath who talked like a musician, soulful, throwin' touchdowns on a bum knee. And don't forget 'The Greatest.' Ali!

The opposite of authority is infantilism. That's what we have a lot of now in the culture.
Jazz was another country, came up off the underground railroad, an invisible world in plain sight, with its own language, customs, rights of passage, codes, membership rituals and sacraments.

Read Mezz Mezzrow, kids!!!

Hip-hop's another world too. Punk's a village, a shifting community. Folk and blues are for loners. Poetry is for the shipwrecked! Sticking messages in a bottle and sending them out to sea, and every hundred years one makes land: HOWL! LEAVES OF GRASS!

Sheesh.

True esoteric knowledge held by youngsters: Bob Dylan knew blues, folk, the Bible, rock & roll, Hank Williams and bluegrass, Beat poetry like Corso, e.e. cummings, American geography and history. He'd written a million unpublished words by the time he was 20. Elvis knew: Gospel, blues, country, R&B and folk, and recombined the elements in a completely original way at Sun Studios when he was 19. And he knew how he wanted it to look, too! Both of these artists were young movie afficionados.

What do you know, folks? When you unpack, is there anything

good in the bag?

The great mushifier: television.

Does the Internet play a similar or different role? Does it enhance life, or suck it dry?

(David Ensminger)

Sometimes when I hear the word musician my muscles tense in my neck and my body chills to the word. It sounds too much like 'refrigerator repairman.' Digging down deep into Lightnin' Hopkins's humidity-infested days of gin and gambling, he might scoff at the word because such guys were the session fellows called in by white record label owners to help soften and channel the cigarette smeared, bony raw, gin-thickened southern grit of the real bluesmen, whose days in the menial cotton fields didn't teach them proper mechanics and language of song, according to book rules and halls of universities. They were the primitive and naïve, the intuitive and superstitious, the screechers and the howlers, the real fellaheen in the merciless heat. Their bent callused fingers invoked another kind of muse.

In the glare of fluorescents and snappy blue ribbon awards and DIY box kits from Borders and endless TV channels, everybody makes everything, and nobody makes anything. People still amass on the border of Sudan and Somalia, in tent cities, raked by devilish dirt, and no one can figure out how to get them enough peanut butter and mosquito nets. Technicians disassemble ICBM missiles, 500,000 people gawk at the last surge of the space shuttle, and all I can do is think of skinny Gil Scott Heron blaring "Whitey on the Moon."

There's no prose stuck midway in the belly of a Tweet. There's no visions of the sublime in the turnstile of emails, the back and forth hemorrhage of e-book business transactions.
Real magic evades and eludes, it refuses to be cornered by pedestrian observations, by the postcard flimsy neurosis of middle-class aspirations. The magic of the vernacular comes in spats, just like Richard Hell looked love square in the eye.

The authority of Sam Charters has become the lifeless, stiffened meditations ala Facebook therapy, the plunge into vapid politics of lies and charades and misquotes.
Artists are no longer the arbiters of taste and intellect; they are simply zipped-lock digital files, cozy and displaced on iPods, dreaming of former analog homes, with speakers big as donkeys in living rooms where people once huddled, dancing shamelessly to Miles Davis on shag carpeting.

People laugh at poetry because they trip over it, they can't eat it like diet shrink-wrapped food, they can't sell it for 150% profit, they can't make it unstuck from its conqueror – the academy.

Burroughs said, always with a smirk and sinister smile, we must "Storm the citadels of knowledge."

In New York City, the citadels beam in steel and glass enclosures, while in the shimmering field of the grain belt, knowledge rests in libraries musty and remote. Burroughs tunneled through history like a shark, like a bulldozer, like a scavenger with shotgun at the ready. Ginsberg quoted from the depths of Karmic manuscripts, Corso shouted in Greek, di Prima held the hand of Sappho. Cy Twombly made his scribbles huge as trees, forked his fingers around the utterances of time unlocked, smattered the paintings with a hefty dose of history made public.

Now we head to Best Buy and long for satellite TV.

Where do we draw from: do we seize an iota of truth from the milligram measured TV blips? Are we afraid to get cultured and lose our pop? Are we afraid to go pop and get shortchanged by the elite?

I'll bite down on Hubert Selby and John Rechy and John Fante and leave Rollins to the legions of TV babies. I'll listen to MDC and the Dicks because they stuffed Hendrix down their hardcore pants when hippies were supposed to be dead and gone.
I'll adore Kathy Acker even when she's terrible, or terribly brilliant, or terribly porno, or terribly obtuse, because she lifted weights and out-punked Patti Smith, and never forgot to bring Catallus, fanzines,

and Genet along in her wolf-bitten dreams.

I'll place my faith in Otis Redding because he still has more rollick in one foot beat, one rasped vowel, one pump-it-up gyration, than most people can conjure in an armchair lifetime.

When I hear infantilism, communism is conjured. Left-Wing Infantilism is what the old yellowed Soviet-style pamphlets used to decry. Perhaps now the infantilism is the fact that everyone steers the wheel of culture, and we are all lost on the highways of bytes and facsimiles. Everybody is an infant in the womb of capitalism.

Luck measures out the fate of the few; the others start clawing and crawling, making their mark as the world fissures around them. The inside beam of street culture means one thing in gay, posh, and eatery-lined neighborhoods and another in the barrio, where the poor still gather in bundles of language, laundry, and old country harvests of sorrows, fears, religion, and intelligence.

I feel 21st century one second, absolutely yanked down into the 19th century in another. I hear the car alarms and the roosters, the aerosol cans and air-conditioning, the rattled dogs and the whir of iMacs. Birds die of thirst on the corner, pools of gasoline-gleaming water mirror their plight. I am waiting for the next Kerouac to saunter in, or Langston Hughes, or the next Pablo Neruda and Kate Chopin...

(PC)

Why can't e-mails contain visions of the sublime? I think they can and do. Tweets are for the birds, but your friend sure liked them a lot. Why?

'Musician' is a holy word, a higher calling for some. But it's the 'hacks' that are the ones brought in to corral the muse-ics wildness, the lames for hire. 'Musicianer': you ever hear that one?

Primitive modern. George Russell talks with Ornette about intuition as 'Third World Technology.' I saw this on YouTube.

"Real magic evades and eludes." Yeah. But this world ain't goin' back for nothin', that's for sure. The 'real world' disappears like a jumbo jet, in a roar and whoosh of incredible rapidity, existent on an electronic grid. Bye bye. The magicians still go on foot.

Peter Ackroyd talks about Blake and **"the long lost secret: the opening of the gate: the sure knowledge that nature and the material world are the vessels of Eternity."**

The world has been reduced to the material, to numbers, to whatever and only what can be codified and sold, for money. The inside beam of street culture, on the other hand, flows for fun and for free, has to know it all, and begins to repair the damage, tho' not necessarily mend all divisions.

JK, Pablo Neruda, worked fucking hard... doubt tho', is like breath.

"The 'real world' disappears like a jumbo jet, in a roar and whoosh of incredible rapidity, existent on an electronic grid. Bye bye. The magicians still go on foot."

(DE)

...the grid, the web, the infrastructure of interlocutors zooming to and fro on the warm addictive buzz -- users skimming the manic plastic and glass eye of materiality under the gaze of weary ghost Kafka, can they capture the magic of those on foot? Can the dead-bolted cargo of made-in-China computers convey magic and otherness; can it prod the dream machine to disconnect us from control? Or does its guise of rapid ceaseless freedom allure us: the magic of digital worlds, of moan bitch complain blogs and syrupy sweet Kodak inspired tweets, of paranoia stretching for miles, of 3-D museums without customers, of music created in garage band isolation disseminated via huge coal-fired plants supplying the grid or silent satellites inhabiting the outer limits like tiny robot moons, of video conferences instead of family meals, of Skype sex and low grade orgasms, until we are bloodless vessels?

Are we hunched over like writers from the 1920s pecking at typewriters louder than bombs? But they ran towards print factories and unions, drinks and ruddy talk, nighttime skies menaced by bugs and tugboat smoke, as we lean back, glazed with the ease of chairs built to keep us medicated.

Is Peter Ackroyd discussing Blake as bard of transcendentalism – the karmic shudder in the eye of God-stuff felt in the purr of wind and shiver of moth wing? Is it the same gates that lead to the Western Lands, is it a rabbit hole, is it where some indigenous tribes ascended from, is it the one that will lead me past Lethe, is it the one that will land me square at the feet of Delphi, or at the rook of Buddha's lap? If the long lost secret is the opening of the gate, if nature and the material world are the vessels of Eternity, is language capable of bearing that truth? Is the key to void-out language … all the poems of Blake no more than wallpaper on consciousness?

"The world has been reduced to the material, to numbers, to whatever and only what can be codified and sold, for money. The inside beam of street culture, on the other hand, flows for fun and for free, has to know it all, and begins to repair the damage, tho' not necessarily mend all divisions."

I dig the inside beam as repair man, as leaky deluge fixer, the reverser of flow, the free stirring democratic ethos of repairing civilization from below, of vitalizing and rejuvenating, or how did Bob Kaufman invoke Lorca: he undid all the numbers but never crossed a dream? I think the meaning finally gels in me.

I just made a haiku in my head, an ode to Robert Creeley, who I saw in Des Moines in 1989, me the only student to linger as the bell rang, his grizzled patient face stretching for a second when I mentioned Ginsberg.

Who shall send me the receipt
for the catalog of my sorrows?

"Doubt tho', is like breath..." and Becket said, Fail again, fail
better. Or as I said, in an ode to Kenneth Patchen, long lost jazz poet,
lover surrealist, better to be a butterfly with no wings than a lizard
with an extra tongue.

Language, despite platform and tools, always contains a kernel of the
sublime, tucked into the recess, the lingering ash of voice thru
hieroglyphics. The symbol, the typeface, the rudimentary byte
cannot extinguish that, no doubt. But it is the manner by which the
emails usually stick to routine habits of usage – emails that scarcely
form thoughts, let alone a kind of prose. It is quick-speak, the code
of busy-ness, the vernacular of technocrats-in-waiting. Some slow
down to let the sublime poke through like needles expanding into
clouds, but most hurry thought the gates of need and desire,
relinquishing creative control.

Tweets are the noise of democracy in action. Instant gibberish for
those, to quote Wordsworth, me thinks, who live in quiet
desperation. The addiction to communication, rather than discussion.
A dive into an ocean of plenitude, where every input feels like a
Greek ruin smattered with graffiti. This is the sound of the folk,
skittering through a hyper-kinetic world. This is the womb of
interconnectedness, the digital reach of voices needing feedback,
playback, and remote controlled attention.

I like the term musicianer, the play on for-hire, the rent-a-cop of the
musical studio and boys with profit eyes. I wouldn't use the label
musician, likely, even if denoting a higher calling, to describe
someone like Albert Ayler: he is artist, bar none. No less. Currently,
the word artist is loaded with an aftertaste of narcissism, or mumbo
jumbo for the elite. But I think we should recoil from anything else.
He is not blowing his way through scales for the sake of soundscan
sales and professional prestige, he immersed in duende, spiritus,
satori, gestalt-rearrangement.

George Russell talking (with … or at?) Ornette about "intuitive
intelligence" as form of 'Third World Technology' stemming from

the heart is interesting. Most of us easily slip into 'language as tool' fixations, but intuition as technology suggests a modern primitivism, if we revert back to intuition, 'first thought best thought,' or the outliers discussed in the book *Blink*. But in that, Malcolm argues 10,000 hours of purposeful practice preclude a "natural" and genuine range of intuition and sharp instant mental acuity/discernment.

Besides the handheld camera, the table caked with items, and Ornette nodding kindly, the more interesting part is the folklore of feedback in the commentary, from the critiques of "modern western music/capitalistic market assumptions" to "analytical accuracy than emotional content." The issue seems very complex and likely should not be divided between upper and lower bodily stratum – heart vs. head – or cerebral vs. emotional. To me, music actually collapses those distinctions all together: it unspools time itself. But I will defer to my friend Thomas Barnett of Strike Anywhere on this one, who sums up some of the underlying facets to the debate:

"Perhaps, as evolutionary psychologists have suggested, the invention of time was a viral idea, suffocating and codifying the richer tapestry of consciousness which our ancestors possessed. Our large brains, and the oft-cited ten percent of them which we only use, could also have had their growth aborted by this invention of a fractured and imprisoned conscious language … I read somewhere once that language itself could be viewed as a patriarchal tool, wrenching a balance of senses used in previous communication arts our species had, carving a narrow path of expression to cripple and contain our biggest thoughts. With each successive language introduced, instead of progressing in further detail and achievement, a circumcision of meaning and interruption of creativity occurs by demanding absolutes from ideas larger than words."

So much to bite, so much to wonder. That's what I miss from the dynamics of modernity, the old-fashioned curiosity cabinets of the mind. Instead, we no longer envision ourselves as amateur explorers, just as edge culture junkies or new age practitioners with Third World awareness -- dudes with 12,000 songs stuffed in the palm of iPod soft hands, divorced from history. If YouTube was a locus of fieldwork that went beyond backyard guffaws and people-as-puppets show, I might watch more.

Modernity has let me down.

Nihlism/ American culture/ materialism/ know nothings-ism?

What IS heavy metal?

Punk rock, A.G.'s "big crybaby"?

Are politics all really of Satan?

People need a payoff.

Nihilism: formerly European's fiery fuel against institutions ... the politics of nothing, no core, no truths, yet a belief nonetheless ... anti-culture writ large in the shadows and history of war and body bags ...

nobody should be pimped to ideas, free agency is the freedom to fuck off ... the narcotic that fueled most of hardcore, the undertow that dragged us into what Lester Bangs called "the womb" of punk's angrier melting pot, boys and girls enveloped in savage fury and loathing, the atavistic arteries of three chords and 122 MPH drum beats.

Know-nothing is different, a willful kind of stupor, of Blake proportions, kids believing in the nothing but things themselves: the taste of lollipop fast food, Twinkie heaven,
TV show prayers, the void of history gaping like a syphilis wound.

Heavy metal is the sound of guitars bending in the night to a tech-savvy belief in wizardry, talent, and musicianship, gore and glam, pretension and nonsense, hallowed riffage and hollow-eyed song fare, the leather triumph and Harley hubris, the myth of rock replete with fascist operas...

punk rock big crybaby more like renegade Mayakovsky reinvented in Western idioms,
not cry baby like fetish John Waters' Baltimore middle class babies, but like cry baby I am all perhaps spectacle no action, or in my book intro me states, I am TV baby birthed in the paws of capitalism, and punk flipped the off button, for me.

Hmmm, politics and the lure of satan: the language of selling truths lacking real gristle or blood? The lexicon of ruse?

You should wear the bracelet: what would Blake do? What would Shelley do? How would DH Lawrence and Henry Miller deal?

Me still believes in some figment and fragment of politics, in micro-form, the choice daily encountered, speaking to the forum, speaking to the stone steps of Greek slave society hungry for food and poetry, the politics of personhood, what drove the Ensmingers from Rotterdam's last smells, that stationed them in Natchez as the gun boats lingered and the slaves clung to the river, that politics that drove Ensmingers to uproot the natives in Ohio but could be used to bring back the people of the mounds and mountains...

poetry needs a payoff, people need a dose of arthouse and old timey tunes, of weddings to moonscapes and money on the plate, of food ripe for bellies and bellies ripe with possibilities: no more dancing with death in the industrial gullet, no more over-abundance of language cured in irony and condescension

(PC):

Nihilism: in the young, a product of despair. Nihilism is for their elders, when the elders have aged unwise, in a false non belief system, and leads to dead end and suicide, for example, Ayler. For example, you can name 'em:

'Destroy all music culture art love political action'... is a tonic, a strategy for an historic moment, but not even really a direction anywhere. It cleans the slate, except the slate never really gets clean, but fills with horror. Abominations of death and self destruction are the end result. Punk rock's nihilism: **Johnny Rotten's 'WE MEAN IT,MAN!" becomes George Bush 41's 'READ MY LIPS!' the ultimate appropriation of style, from death, to death.**

"Living in the solution" is what they say in 12 step programs... came to believe. **"You gotta believe"- the 69 Mets!** Compulsory angry negativism just as lame as pollyanna nonsense.

Somebody made the point about Miles that both the be-bop harmonic changes jazz and the atonal music he played were European: Western. Afro/Eastern tribal music is where he found the freedom and beauty he'd sought. Another way to go, outside of the old conundrums of head/heart, tonal/atonal...

Heavy metal is where stupid **unimaginative forms of male energy** found THEIR rock: a codified meassage of death the only one possible, the voice of a culture hopelessly addicted to money, ignorance, class murder, fans bamboozled by corporate powers, confusing volume with strength, power with grace, the music played at CIA torture parties, rev up the bloodlust. And that's always what it's been for... then ingested into mainstream culture, OF COURSE... it so accurately apes it.

Evil IS Evil? Yes or no? Slayer is good for the kids, their fans? A healthy
"escape." I'm against the worship of death, whether on a festival stage or at the Vatican. Dumb yucks are for squares. Ozzy is a square. King Diamond is a square. Judas Priest, square for squares.

There has, historically speaking, always been a lot of squares.

Who wants to FEEL?

And I don't really buy Burroughs/ Gysin's write-off of language. It silenced Ginsberg for a couple seasons there. Of course, with every medium, you give something for what you get, right?

Yeah, I'm still there, discourse, politics, but it's all a lie now.

Search and repair.

(DE)

Off to gig, but first:

Nihilism as couture – style and pose of mannequins -- beliefs as empty signifiers. Nihilism as tonic, as huge sedative crunching the frontal lobe, a mother's little helper, a killer buzz. Nihilism as highway inside negative space, a mantra of rubber manna, a supposed way to tune out the false tongues. Nihilism as method to rewire the network, exposing the ideologues as idiots. Nihilism as the death urge, exposed by you as sham.

The historic moment folded inward until nothing more than a codex of men that once gripped Camus novels and wept for Gide.

The slate is always slick with the blood of the powerless; the slate is nothing more than Sisyphus' dilemma. Roll that nihilism up the hill boy, but I still profit off every inch.

"We mean it, man," I once thought was a torpedo of truth. We mean nothing, the exact inversion.

The map lined up by Oscar Wilde. Only the shallow know themselves, and Johnny Rotten was the leer of the shallow, a jukebox lad, a fractured T-shirt of a boy spun out in the wet dreams of a former Teddy wear proprietor.

Compulsory negativism was the trademark of heroin punk – the shattered bone marrow of music left over from the sliced and diced arms of people living in rat motels. Gingivitis mallpunk.

Didn't Miles get the atonal from the likes of "Rites of Spring," from the avant-garde denizens of white music halls?

To me, the most important Eastern phenomena is not scales and notes and tonality but rhythm. The East's beat does not live in the same box, at all. Rock'n'roll was the hammer and mallet. The East presented the clusterfuck and the constellation, the Elvin Jones soundtrack to the heart.

Heavy metal is the cock of death, yet the splatter urge is controlled like a mouse in a maze. Though Slayer soldiers pounded rounds into Iraqi villages, like terror-spiel, *Combat Rock* set off the Gulf War in a funk-punk purge.

The blood lust of soccer hooligans, 25,000 Metallica fans singing "Kill Em All,"
like a Nuremberg costume party of the macabre, all plumb the same Nietschean veins.

The voice of yearning power emanating in every direction of the trailer park, in the backwoods and barrios alike. King Diamond rising from his fake coffin, like 1930's Hollywood, Alice Cooper backwash, but Judas Priest, despite their mythic metal jargon and walls of oversized amps and monster truck fireworks, remains subversive queer S&M on some level....

(PC)

It's hot as chloroform and I can't sleep my way out of a wet bag
dreams of donkeys tortured and vast seasides
bring me up with three quick shouts and I'm back
through the crack in the barbwire wrack on glass
to my own bedroom prison cathode boredom moto-cycle
enterprise landing pad of saturn desperation

wishing I had a language that hung to my knees
my stomach and my crotch have switched juices
kneed in the groin kay-ode pay owed see? oh D.

a skunk crunk uncle with some punk sunk junk
whooda thunk? up an' outta muh bunk:
a clunk that stunk a lunk outta his funk

like monk.

SONG

I'm a dinosaur
just learned how to mambo
i'm headin' to the congo
buddy can you spare a dime?

shy like chicken little
drownin' in my spittle
i'll take this chance to whittle
a plea for my aquittal.

(DE):

By the time the 1970s hit like a decade of endless war and
technocracy, last cough of old-timey industrial America with drunk
factory floor picnics in the park, in the unblinking
eye of feminism and soiled Marxist dreams as terrorist chic became
the new norm, in the fetid music business trying to rehash the
crooners and pop and country gone 'politan
and faux hillbilly in Green Acres jokeville, in the poetry society
boredom and beatnik survivalist communes in beggar cities and
fecund farms, Burroughs came like a menace, bearing the Word as
act of sabotage and release.

His cut-up plowed through the mysticism of Om, plowed through the jargon of manuals, plowed through typescript of *New York Times*, plowed through the soft melodies of the Beatles, plowed through plastic middle-class supermarkets...

Ginsberg was at a loss, me thinks. The hard fecund prose and evocative skits of *Naked Lunch*, with its peripheral narrative, had given way to soft boys and exploded tickets. Given way to ART, cold-shouldered and autonomous, print treated as no more than expendable source of games. Glue, scissors, and pasted words: the forbearer to punk flyers. There was no more Isadora Duncan, no more Walt Whitman catalogs of Americanspeak. Progressive America had given way to the men's movement, yogurt counters at the mall, and one last howl at the Republicans.

Burroughs was the ultimate doctor of language, clinical and precise, completely mechanized at times, though still with an instinct of wordplay borne of ennui.

No wonder Ginsberg turned to the blues even deeper, soon saddened at punk rock's choleric cough and hate-body urge. Joe Strummer's style had been paved earlier than most punks in squat rot and Woody Guthrie gumption. He who wanted to be both Scorcese and Ginsberg, not some punk progeny stuck on redux. Strummer the cockney cowboy player, the worker of the world strummer, the warbly throated testifier...

(PC):

Saturday night, Santa Monica. Denise ran out to her friend's house. I'm sittin' here in my underwear, at bare lightbulb kitchen table, it's hot as hell and humid, too... guess you know all about it over there in Houston, but sheesh! Old scratched up Charlie Patton album on the turntable. I'm drinkin' a cup of PG tips tea. You ever have that? I bought it at the Indian grocery, the one where they make the great jackfruit, over on Washington Blvd, in Venice. It's good tea, strong, good with some honey and soymilk. Why am I drinking something hot? Well, that's a heatwave strategy I can dig: it'll feel so good when I quit, ha!

Why did we start diggin' these guys? What's the point? Man, I loved
this: "Dog," by Lawrence Ferlinghetti as a 13 year-old kid:

The dog trots freely thru the street
and the things he sees
are smaller than himself
Fish on newsprint
Ants in holes

Chickens in Chinatown windows Warning to kiddies: whoever you start diggin' as a child is gonna be revealed to be human at some point, and human means: problems. It's just the way it is. Ginsberg became a dirty old man. Burroughs became increasingly more paranoid and less graceful about it. His opinions became less incisive. See the last Naropa journal Ann Waldman put together if you don't believe me (by the way, her poem in the Beat Reader Ann Charters put together, Our Past, wow). Shotgun art? I dunno... he stayed far out, you gotta hand that to him. Kerouac dies of Terminal Drunk, lives with his mom his whole life. Corso? A heroin addicted womanizing con-man. Neal Cassady: run over counting railroad ties, bombed, in Mexico, in his mid-forties.

Who you gonna dig? Life knocks us down, the heroes keep gettin' back up, but it ain't no zero sum game. Flesh and blood, lordy, flesh and blood! Brain cells to boot! Years of loneliness, ornery, hauling visions, rising on dream ladders? In the pain of rejection, taunted by the ignorant, leveraged by the rich, browbeaten by landlords after years of no pay... 'cause poetry is not an upwardly mobile existence. You START at the top, and either angelize, or work your way down, or both.

Dylan is a phenomenon, the great poet of our hundred years, a carrier of the message, ALL THE WAY from BLAKE, DANTE, WILLIAM TYNDALE, SHAKESPEAR, KEATS, RIMBAUD, VERLAINE, etc... POE, MELVILLE, DICKINSON, HART CRANE, ETC ETC.... TO ::::::::::::::::::: the aformentioned BEATS to:: US! You and me, pal... and the reader. Dig it.

By the way dig this by Alice Notley:
Jack Would Speak Through The Imperfect Medium Of Alice
So I'm an alcoholic Catholic mother-lover/yet there is no sweetish nectar no fuzzed-peach/ thing no song sing but in the word/to which I'm starlessly unreachably faithful

Here's Ann Waldman:

Our Past

...You had traveled back from Utah
I thought of the Salt Lakes, seeing them once from a
plane they were like blank patches in the mind or
bandaged places of the heart
I felt chilly

Is that heartbreaking GREAT or what?
Lord have mercy...

(DE)

The night fades into a dismal yellow across ozone city. The heat makes every joint feel enervated, not a muscle ready to plow into the PM. Leaning back in a black metal poc-marked chair, slurping the last traces of yogurt, like some kind of soft pornography on the tongue, I shift my mind back into the VHS screen time of 1989, when I was leaving high school for a school sitting squat in the doldrum city of Des Moines. Soon I would write a poem, sometime before or after my march on Washington, that summed up the gist of my feelings:

"Iowa"
Miles and miles of corn / that I will never eat

There is a toy box the size of fat pig in my parent's basement, til this day, containing the scraps of my writing. Eggheaded attempts at Edgar Allen Poe, woe and gloom poems more befitting bands like Bauhaus. Early 6th grade in-house published movie criticism, so earnest and terrible and cock-eyed. Bits of gangster lore, on yellow legal paper. A biography of Johnny Rotten, written from the slanted view of a fifth grader.
By the time I left for Iowa's meat packing plant socialist teach-ins and radio station guffaw and video channel MTV wanna-be talent pool, I had two bookcases stuffed with
novels and poetry, another with records, and a pile of New Directions paperbacks, slim as a dime it seems, each preaching a kind of poesy considered esoteric, old-fashioned, blundered, soft-bellied by most people around me chewing on hardboiled dimestore fiction.

The Jim Thompsons and Bukowskis, novels about heart aches and fisticuffs, staring at the bottom of a gin bottle or betting on lean horses. Ferlinghetti came to me like a Paul Revere, yelling "the squares are coming," the people void of wits and history, and I'd better clench down and get ready for a life of the body electric that only a handful of people could adjust to, figure out, enjoy, or mimic.

Ferlinghetti like a backyard prophet or sage, but who looked more like a longshoreman at times. Books like *Who Are We Now?* don't even need pages. The photo of the Ferlinghetti scrawling graffiti, in some ode to the heady French students and situationalists, to American urban argot, was enough. But to pry back the cover and actually read the early 1970's prose, with its endless tropes of outsiderness and left-winger loudness and odes to Bob Dylan and Jack Kerouac, its mounds of parallel phrases, it spokenness and Bibleness, its oeuvre of oratory, borrowed I suppose from distant players like Kenneth Rexroth and Maxwell Bodenheim and Vachel Lindsay, resonated:

who are we now, who are we ever?

skin, books, parchment, bodies, libraries of the living.

He steered the wheel towards belief. There is a secret undertow to America, and it exists no more distinct than bread makers or mechanics. America is steeped in letres, even in deep down petroglyph America, aboriginal and ancient, in which porous rock is the parchment. Mayakovksy was a culture worker, Ginsberg was a culture worker, Anselm Hollo, Jaques Prevert too, all the imprint of New Directions and City Lights, containing all the Pasolinis of poetry. Tell me the names of the culture workers today, the prose-benders printing the books that are the backbone of the counterculture...

(PC):

This is all inspirational. Your letters deserve more than me throwing a few riffs back at you. I respond to every word in this, nearly every sentence opens up into another world of associations. Black Metal Pocked Mark Chair. Soft Porn Yogurt. Midwest Haiku. That one on the previous letter, about the receipt. Scraps of Writing in a Fat Pig Toy Box. Johnny Rotten's Fifth Grade Bio. "The squares are coming..." Some books don't need pages.

Ferlinghetti was the one who really kicked it all off for me. When I got to SF I used to see him running up and down in front of the store, coming and going, busy, in and out, an American hero. City Lights and New Directions, yeah man, getting things DONE.
Now?

Rollins? He may have been doing it. A lot of people have a start on it, but maybe no one's working hard enough, IN THE RIGHT WAY. It's all about PRODUCT now, selling the stuff on the road. That's the only network. Robert Cantwell's books on music are great, but academic. "If Beale Street Could Talk.' Robert Palmer was a great writer about music, and he died too soon. Bly had a few great moments, though he began to fool up, and dropped out. I dunno, there's a lot of pilgrims. Hard to say, it's such a noisy press out there.

But I dig what yr sayin.

Yeah, I know, it ain't Rollins. He's done something, but what adds up? No counter culture? Just front counter check out lines.

No one's spreadin' the word. Point of view ain't the same as image. Poetry ain't just piles of words, waiting to be spread on dry loaves of white bread.

Mash ups are (or were) thrilling the hipsters---hipsters that ain't hip to shit. Noam Chomsky is right, and so bloodlessly boring. wtf lol pos fu kma ok?

But what about IOU? IOU the truth? IOU the effort? IOU a lucky break like the one I got? IOU the best I've got to give til I drop?

Do IOU my soul?

Rollins has become a con-a-sewer, thinks it's about him, and the rewards of minor stardom.
But at least he played Minor Threat on the radio in LA. Fugazi sounded like a machine, music for the senseless. I guess that's the point. Fugazi was muscular without being moving, to my ears. MT had it all going, what happened to them?

Punk was the counterculture that failed. After the hippies tripped, and before hip-hop flip flopped. And the culture workers vanished up all those spouts.

Which brings us full circle, back to the dock.

What is a musician? An artist? A culture worker?

Myriads climbing.

I gotta take a break now, going back on tour tomorrow, home again in a week...

(DE):

No doubt that the Midwest, for me, carves a steep sense of getting things done. My own Dad yelling furiously if a yard tool sat all night in the prim front yard grass, speckled with potential rust freckles. Dad yelling if I didn't mow the lawn in the right direction, different every time, so the yard looked mint and unused, postcard serene, plastic as turf in a football stadium.

Dad yelling to dig up the weeds and bury the dead guinea pig. To hit more baskets with the ball, move my skinny ass, use my wrists, huffing and puffing, trying to prevent my arcing shots though he's inches short, me riffing in my head like Jim Carroll without the dead friends clinging to me. Dad taking my Xerox nation fanzines to work after-hours, letting the bulky machine whirl with photos of hardcore punk mutiny or anxious poems styled on City Lights pocketbooks and their catalog of disruption and foment. The Dad of hobby store mornings and Jewish neighborhoods, thick lens glasses and Army teaching gigs in grueling El Paso and Missouri trailer parks.

How do we get things DONE like Amiri Baraka denouncing his own old name and forging the chapbooks of heresy and committing to the leftist network, spinning poems in a tongue that feels as multi-tendril'd as a Coltrane Ayler blow-out. What happened to the large sense of art-tonomy, the riffing on autonomy, the cocoon of community, the methods to break the ennui of late-capitalism deadlock?

City Lights was epicenter, Gotham Books was epicenter, record stores were epicenters, is Amazon epicenter, an algorithm of art-autonomy? Is it just a commodity pit stop on the information expressway? A florescent way station in the bumpy road of desire? Is blogging the terminus that reinvents the chapbook or a just a future dead site, floating in the dark matter of the digital world? To hold the books of the beats was to hold the key, to flip the switch, to inflame the flame, to penetrate the plastic sheen and dig up the old America of letres.

It was an archeology of angst old as midnight in Boston harbor, old as the grit of Crispus Attucks, old as the Appalachian Indians displaced by whites carrying imported songs and rifles.

What happened to the American elegies, the codex of memory and longing to connect, the poem-form millennium old, Catallus coughing? Poems like "Elegiac Feelings American," Corso's long-lost scribbles for Kerouac, or Ginsberg's odes to Frank O'Hara and Vachel Lindsay, poets that do not sit well with Starbucks' prepackaged meals, or do they?

Or Ginsberg's paramount pen stroke to Whitman, "What thoughts I have of you tonight...gray beard, lonely..." Is this the America you dreamed of, he asks, I ask, likely you ask, putting our faith in history, character, and inevitable destiny to the test.

Whitman got things DONE. He built the houses, he soothed and bandaged the soldiers, he took his brother's arm, he flashed the President his whiskers, he rewrote his material every ten years, he became the father of Garcia Lorca who became the father of Bob Kaufman who closed his mouth in lieu of Buddha and dead presidents...

Whitman drew up elbow to elbow with Ezra Pound who finally caved in to him. He sang the worker songs the soldier songs, the gay Louisiana songs. He capitalized on the language of an industry that could build bridges spanning mosquito islands turned Barnaby financial districts while starving black men in southern fields sang; he saw the body electric as America went electric...

Rollins certainly compelled me at one time. I stole the the title of my fanzine *No Deposit No Return* from him, but then he became another Lydia Lunch, a "transgressive" with first-bite appeal but offered me no longer roads or dimensions. Now, listening to any post-1983 Black Flag sometimes makes my spine squirm.

How do we get the things DONE? American youth once created an empire of Xerox, a paper city avant-garde, via snail mail and record store corkboards and street poles, fomented in fury and finesse that most of the Louvre would at least smile at, but the digital nation makes them tokens of tree killing and quaint parchment, like LP fetishists. There's more thrust and humanity and lore in hand-painted signs dangling from every broken pole and slanted barber shack in

America than Photobucket could ever stomach.
Kerouac's America is still there, dwindling only in total breadth, but plenty of places loom in the backside of America.

As you saw, even blocks away from skyscraper skylines resides a lowdown America, a boarded up America, a no air conditioning America, sweating in balmy exhaust fumes. University poems don't speak there. Does Lightnin' speak there? Or does crunk? Does the radio still belt out? Or does the iPod blink? Does the cassette tape still exist, or does the memory of Memorex? Who will try to erase our tapes?

(PC):

Thelonious Monk: Advice

Transcribed by Steve Lacy who played with Monk in the 1960's.

-- The inside of the tune (the bridge) is the part that makes the outside sound good.

-- Don't play everything (or every time); let some things go by. Some music just imagined. What you don't play can be more important that what you do.

-- A note can be small as a pin or as big as the world, it depends on your imagination.

-- When you're swinging, swing some more.

(DE):

Got your phone message...
It's our anniversary...
But wanted to send this...
Keep writin', if only behind your eyelids.

The Monk list reminds me of Kerouac's list "Essentials of
Spontaneous Prose," which I tacked up in my apartment in a 1873
building in downtown Rockford, next to the old Victorians blocks
somehow unscathed. I had Xerox pictures of Voznesensky,
a postcard of Edgar Allen Poe's cellar apartment in Philadelphia,
Xeroxed portraits of Mayakovsky and Bill Burroughs.

Thinking back to the Lou Reed elegies, song cycles dissecting
cancer, cancer described by Louis Erdrich in her devastating poem
about John Wayne as an invasive force, doubling/splitting out of the
cells in a mutiny against the skin, cancer as doppleganger for the
Hollywood-meets-Manifest Destiny actor: "Even his disease was the
idea of taking everything." Tim gone, Kathy now gone too.

What happens to place when it gets pounded into void, a
concrete glass plastic building facing the wrong side of the
sun? Place, like I mentioned yesterday, place. Kenneth Rexroth said,
"Must have a place. Dog has a place." I suppose he was not being
simply geo-physical, he was engaging the fact that we must know
where we fit. I found that quote in an early 1990s paper I wrote
while living in Santa Fe, across from heroin-soaked adobe alley. The
dry-baked mesquite old pine nut America where the A-bomb secrets
were traded on a rickety bridge, where O'Keefe's vulva flowers stole
their sunlight, and I nearly followed Gene Hackman into the
bathroom to get an inside scoop of Tinsel City.

I found this paper jutting out of a box this morning, while the light
burst angry and hot against the window. I tried to tell my instructor,
a man of linebacker girth from Notre Dame, that Patchen delved into
place, meaning, and identities, zeroing in on frontline matters. I think
back to the word body yesterday: I neglected to mention. Body is
book. I always believed that.

Speech or writing must invoke physicality to some degree. Barthes called it "throwing … the anonymous body of the actor into my ear." Pound used a different dictum: poetry that strays too far from music atrophies. The music is the body. Beat heart beat. The body is the instrument. Book too must be body. Artaud knew this too well: the theater must be cruel to the body to set it free. Kerouac's *Blues and Haikus* knows that poems, even haikus, must be attached to body, the blues a kind of extension of body, the wear and tear making the soundtrack possible to blues.

Phrase groups align naturally to body in the jazz-spiels of Langston Hughes. Kerouac fused/blended music into books, the perfect timing of the adroit phrase, intricate effects of timing and intonation.

Have you ever read *Civilization and Its Discontents* by Freud -- he mentions the three directions that threaten us: our own bodies ("doomed to decay and dissolution," said with the alliteration of a poet in the arms of psycho-science), the external world (is this the thread that the naturalists/realists knew, the Stephen Cranes?) and our relationship to other men -- which he insists is perhaps more painful than the others.

Without place, without sense of body, the third becomes an even heavier burden, heavier threat, heavier anguish. Perhaps as Kerouac faded from Big Sur's shore, as he fattened into bloated French Canadian mid-life lassitude, as his beatniks became peaceniks, he could he no longer throw his body onto the page. What did he become a doppelganger for?
Did he make body music until the end? That punch in the gut he suffered at the local dive bar near the end, was that a last rite for his body, right beneath his beat heart beat?

(PC):

Back from tour, home until September. I've been going pretty hard since March, so it's a good time for a break. It's gonna take some adjustment: I'll feel like getting up and driving a few hundred miles tomorrow, I just know it!

This last run had me doing a month of one nighters in Europe, then a dozen or so dates in Northern and Southern California, followed by a show in Arizona, four in Texas (great to see you and Julie!) then wrapping up with a transcontinental flight, three days in North Carolina, then immediately another transcontinental plane flight back to the Northwest, straight into three days in Washington State, then home. The gigs have been going great: you play every night like this and it either destroys you or you get in the groove… so, I grooved.

I've been listening to jazz on the drives: Miles, Bird, Monk, Prez, Duke, The Hawk, Charlie Christian with Bennie Goodman and Lionel Hampton. Coltrane, Sun Ra, Mingus, Ornette, Rashan, Sonny Rollins, Dexter Gordon, Herbie, Cannonball. Bill Evans. Sidney Bechet. Louis Armstrong. Jelly Roll Morton. Sarah, Billie, Ella… Ray. Frank. Archie Shepp, Cecil Taylor, Pharoah Sanders. Gil Evans. George Russell. Van Vliet.

It's a lot about tone. Just like all singing, and writing. So that's where I'm at. I'm not gonna do a jazz record or anything. But I'm planning on doing something far out ok? Everybody plays it safe these days… I just want to be myself, and that's what all these cats did: found their own voice in the thick of jazz culture, which is like a whole nation unto itself.

Coltrane was trying to BE REAL. Sing in a REAL VOICE, find musical TRUTH. It's not just bs. It's a lot of work to create BEAUTY. Remember hearing about that? Kind Of Blue. Sketches Of Spain. A Love Supreme. Bringing the people something back from a trip to the other side. It takes time, courage, inspiration, luck, work… it's not about some three line review from a loudmouth in an online music column, who can't even get the idea of the instrumentation he just heard right. I had a guy today say he liked the 'washtub bass' on 'Let's Turn This Thing Around' on the Case Files LP. There ain't no washtub on that, or anywhere near that, ok? The dude doesn't know what he's talking about, but he's gotta talk. He's not even doing it for the money: he's just doing it to hear his own voice I guess. I'm sick of it, this whole culture of democratic bs.

It's worse about the politics. 'The Debt Crisis' : what a fucking load: IT'S A RECESSION, YOU SHITHEADS!!! THE GOVERNMENT SHOULD BE SPENDING, RE-BUILDING, EMPLOYING PEOPLE, PUTTING MONEY IN CIRCULATION!!! That's the way to save us... FDR!!! FDR!!! FDR!!! NOT RONNIE'S BS.

We're in for it though, 'cause nobody is making sense out there. Not the T.P. Not the Dems. Not Obama. The real crisis is coming, mark my words. You can't bullshit real problems forever. Health care is eating us up, and it hasn't been solved. Single payer was THE WAY. Sorry folks, it's true, Dean knew it, and he got run out of the elections... by CORPORATE MONEY.

WHO OWNS THE SUPREME COURT?? Corporate America, 5 to 4. We're screwed as a people until that turns. No honest recourse. Forget your checks and balances. Unlimited corporation money is legal now in elections. Bye bye USA until that gets solved, ok?

I have mixed emotions about being home. Touring is hard, but it's great. I get burned out, but also very inspired. The travel is a bitch. The people are great. I love playing. I love writing too, that's what I'll be doing here.

Aw man, I'm beat. Good night. More on all of this later.
(hours later: couldn't sleep!)

My Dad dug Goodman, Armstrong, Hampton etc. Swing was what they called it. It's jazz. Never dreamt I'd be diggin' it. I mean, I always liked it a little, but it's killin' me now that I dig where it's coming from, and how it leads into the wild '50s and '60s jazz, and beyond. It's an important part of a long and intense story. The story of jazz. And the story of jazz could be... the story of the twentieth century in America.

34

I guess I never really even listened to all these recordings though, they really rock, I can hear where Chuck Berry was inspired (as he says he was) by Charlie Christian. Chuck said that's what he really wanted to play, when he was making all those hits.

My daughter asked me in a phone text what North Carolina was like and I said: "They grow tobacco, race stock cars, eat bar-b-que, and play bluegrass.'

She said, "Sounds awesome!"

In Seattle: "They wear flannel shirts, eat seafood, drink espresso, and play heavy metal," unless "They shoot dope, eat hotdogs, sleep under bridges, and dye their hair."

In LA: "People write scripts, drive in traffic jams, wear ankle bracelets, and riot." They also "Suffer earthquakes, surf, appear in reality shows, and get divorced."

In Texas: "Folks drive pickups, wear boots, eat Mexican food, and handle snakes" unless "They drink beer, stand out front and smoke, dig polkas, and laugh."

I don't know. Up in Buffalo, where I'm from: "People eat pizza, play football, have bad haircuts, and fight." Also, "They yell a lot, ask if 'youse can do d'warsh', go to wrestling at the aud, and love Hillary Clinton."

Not sure I'm on to anything here. Oh well. I'll get back to you.

(DE):

The deadpan drizzle shimmers here like melted bits of aluminum. The roads become clogged and thronged, bulldozers tear the asphalt up in front of Mucky Duck like prying open the chest of the modern city, with its gurgling rot-smell underbelly.

I am aided and abetted on the road by John Lee Hooker's jumpin' "Dimples," which kept my eyes focused on the yellow lines -- then soothed by the gravel-songbird Marianne Faithful. I never know where to place her. Maybe Tin Pan Alley punk, empress of ennui, the sister morphine calling us to bed.

Ventured to Austin to sell the book. Tho attendance was solid at my event at the couture underground bookstore, the money was skinny and sparse. The manager told me that less "discretionary" income flew through his door, yet the city itself reeks of yuppie money these days, only a distant cough of its old self. It feels like Portland with more hygiene and techno-colored dreams. It's the dawn of nu Texas, the next Dallas, as Julie dubs it.

I keep thinking of you as I dig through piles of discount jazz CDs, the floundering infrastructure of the jazz culture nation. Who buys these collections, anyone under 35? All these titanic players reduced to volume discount at the half price store. The complete idiom at odds with modern marketing -- buy today, light up your life ... with Archie Shepp? Even' Hampton's milder grooves barely find a place on satellite radio, where Marky Ramone sounds bored and befuddled by his new role.

I spent almost an hour with Mike Watt, restless and sometimes on the edge of coherence, squirming around his dark backstage room at an awful glitz/glam rock wannabe club ten years ago in the hospital-meets-highway underpass downtown corridors of blinking light Houston. Mike taking of his shirt, still shivering from his near death, grooving on the hopeful blood and bounty contained in each burst/refrain of Coltrane, the ghost of D. Boon measuring his words, photo propped up in guitar case. Just a few weeks ago the old drummer of Lightnin' told me that he wasn't "into" folk like Elvin Jones, whom he never considered as a type that holds down a finite groove with fluidity but much more of a loose, freestyle noisemaker. A drum skin insurgent.

But when I look into the spaghetti-fingered Elvin, the way his fidget wrists turn into blurs and the beat is as deep-delving as Africa unbound, I see terrible exultant beauty ... riffs akin to James Joyce, fractals in human flux form. He doesn't play, he invokes, he makes, he harnesses, he dreams. The method may be maddening to some, but it is the ultimate defiant form of democratic music -- the freedom etched in each downstroke.

Rock'n'roll is Stalinistic, unless you're Pere Ubu; jazz is otherness, when done through these tropes. When unshackled.

This whole culture of 'Must Produce Immediate Digestible Content' becomes the idiom of idiocy. When looking back at *Creem* reviews of the Ramones 1970s, I note the serious ogling of history and art, the need to stay put for a moment and press the ear deeply into the barbarism of each buzzsaw tune. Now, even well-meaning writers are little more than sub-species in the industry, tiny mouthpieces in the Android bazaar, the voice-spiel of multitudes melting into the gibber jabber night.

They hear everything and nothing. All words become weightless facsimiles, empty signifiers. "Strange Fruit" becomes no more than a remix to-be, a centerpiece in the quaint iPod archive. But no one can write the song anymore. No one can write "God Save the Queen" even. No one can hang on the telephone.

The more people get revved up about American debt, the more I eyeball Greece and Italy. In the biography of Artaud, agitator Artaud keenly observes visiting German noir/expressionistic urban spaces prior to WWII; he even heckled Hitler in a cafe.
Former middle-class citizens turned beggars reached out their white arms, the rich became more delirious in their excess and decadence, and the forces of State Authority bolstered their programs and plans.

What would Blake say about the drones hovering over killing fields, what would Orwell say about data mining, what would Huxley say about the doors of perceptions these crooked days?

Is textese the virus of multinationals? Or is it the path, the route, to French Commune-style street fighting for justice measured in milliseconds? Your family text-messages in regards to places are festive and slightly ironic, subversive postcards!

I wish Texas handled snakes instead of the Christian wheels of over-sized SUVs, even as the fashion of such autos disappeared last decade...
Do Californians get divorced while surfing in sitcoms as earthquakes shake their satellite TVs?

38

(PC):

The quiet voice says **"dig the range where sailors dance on twinklegrass and eye the weight of heaven. This is in Washington State, off Highway 90..."**

The words become hard to follow, fade into silence, which is a truckstop blanket of rubber and stone. All is lost again, if only for the time being.

What kind of people destroyed the Native American tribes? Take a look around you, at the 'Indian John Hill Rest Area'. This was the sight of some of the most brutal heartbreaking violence in history, against innocents, until the day we dropped the atom bomb on Japanese women and children. We are the only nation to ever use nuclear weapons. And we did it twice.

Fear is our teacher, our spiritual leader. dishonor and death our traveling companions. Wise up America! Begin to leave your fears behind, okay? You can start the process with little ones: tell somebody what you really think!

"Wisdom? Who cares? Poetry? So what. Beauty? ...in Playboy. Drama? Yr killin' me."
No god in materialist world. No spirit either, and no soul. It all seems obvious to the atheist, but nothing could be further from the truth. "I know there's a god cause he's out to get me."

You can't have something from nothing, but if you did, that's a miracle.

Buddhism's tired truths. Christianity's over excited claims. Which way to go? Lines of traffic on the way to Seattle.

A summer day passing like a ghost in the pines. For all its brightness, fleet. Even the mountains are saying goodbye goodbye goodbye, worn down like sand castles at the beach. I'm in a hurry, want to catch a plane at Seatac, gotta get home, I got my own life to disappear into, to vanish like the sand. The sunshine is so bright, sweet like honey, sweet like a hymn last Sunday. Memories of love

39

won't last you 'til you get some, trust me. Gotta make connections. Write. Forget all those books. Talk about it. Jazz on the CD player, a good day from 1959, Miles, Coltrane, Bill Evans, Paul Chambers, all dead and gone. Kind Of Blue.

Fake politics. Debt crisis? No, just a way for the rich to evade taxes, and express their disdain of anyone with the guts to survive poverty with a mind intact. Taxes? It's called 'society', people. The more fortunate help pay the bills for all, 'cause they've gotten more. Government? That's where the people pool some money they can use to protect themseves from the corporate feeding frenzy.

I'm old, tho' still young enough for joy, some kicks, but gettin' there hurts in ways I never imagined, back when I was 21, takin' on the world and my dreams with a hunting party called the Nerves. In the words of Cleopatra, "blow it out your asp." Do you see what mean? Where was I? The voice is nearly extinguished, for the nonsense give and take of disgracebook.

Seattle? Mountains? Jazz? America? Think I'll go get some coffee.

"Time for tea and meet the wife." First day back. Running up and down them same old fur lined streets, doin' fool's work, gettin' things done that need it, I guess. Leavin' the car radio off, no music, lettin' me hear the sunshine, smell the traffic, taste the palm fronds blowin' in the methadrine wind of beach side So Cal, Santa Monica, things are quite clean here. In certain obvious ways.

In other ways not so much.

Caught in the troughs of commerce, I mean the streets of our town, or any town, from here to Paris, it's all the same deal, money calls the numbers around the world. From shoeshines to sandblasts, acupuncture to soft water therapy, it's all here for those who throw the green. You and me, workin' hard, and buyin' crap with our paychecks. And whatever adventures, trysts, blasts, experiences, visions, epiphanies, and sensations you deliver upon your own nervous system, it's a free country, and it's all up to you.

But everything streetside is on a cash basis.

I tour playing music for a living, have done for years and years. It used to be the records mattered, (and they still do to me and a few others), but basically for most people they seem like an adjunct to the concert line, now. Once upon a time music was a gateway to the forbidden world, to magic, the invisible, to danger too... and the extant to which that is still true is a measure of its worth as a calling. It can't be about the money. It's gotta be about love, spells, the feel, where you get 'em, secret knowledge, turning the world around, freedom, true escape and redemption, or there's no point in playing it, and less than no point for people to listen.

Everyday I'm alive and on the road is a day I'm not in High School. I'm 57 and STILL thankful for that fact. Man, I hated that jive! Starin' out the window of a second story high school classroom, at the traintracks I wished I was walkin' down, towards anywhere... cars goin' by on daytime journeys I wasn't allowed to even know. I dropped out at the first opportunity and I still get a kick out of my freedom, everyday I'm out rollin' on the way to a gig somewhere, its always a plus.

America as the ground I've come to know, all the way around, East to West, North on down to the Gulf, Florida and Texas. Alaska. Hawaii. Mexico itself.

I was thrilled by my first glimpse of the cities on the road. Cleveland, like a futuristic underwater nightmare, Kansas City looming up in the distance as I drive across the plains... ancient looking, with boxcars stretched out a thousand miles across the twilight, baseball games in the summer evening, sand lot and little league, big league stadiums too, lit up like flying saucers.

Cars and late night diners, all night gas, along the freeways, money changing, everywhere you seem, coca cola and texaco.

You can travel in that environment and have NOTHING happen. Ever. A sterile life, carried on in the troughs of commerce, never sloshing the sides, just rolling like a pinball along the path you've charted, or rather, has been charted for you. You can even be GOOD and do that.

41

Like Bob Dylan said: **"It ain't nothin' just to walk around and sing. You have to step out a little, right?"**

And like Keith Richards said: **"We don't talk about this music 'cause it's good. We talk about it 'cause it's GREAT!"**

Sex and drugs were a big part of it. Playing, unraveling the mysteries of music, everynight, singing while you look people in the eye, feeling what's moving the room, and what stirs something inside of you remains the greatest gift. Gambling is part of it. Seeing this great big beautiful world and the people in it, talking to folks, is a gift, too. The miles. Listening to music out there alone on the world.

Lonely hotel rooms become a way of life. Make sure you get some sleep, there's a long drive tomorrow, and no one else to drive it.

The relationships with other musicians you meet, and run into over and over again, through the years on the road, and friends all over the country, staying at houses, meeting their families, seeing how they live.

Every so often something very strange happens, that you try to figure out for years.

And all this goes into the songs, the books, the dreams, and everything you touch. Along with lore of the legends, Woody, Lightnin', Big Joe, Cisco, and Sonny and the gang, along with them our own lore builds up: a hotel jam session with Guy Clark in Georgia, writing songs with John Prine in Nashville in the middle of some nights, running into Dave Alvin in Spokane, he comes in after a LONG drive with his band, sayin "I'm feelin' this one, man." Makin' up songs with Allen Ginsberg on the streets of SF.

The house full of pigs, meeting Springsteen, or taking a crowd out of the club and down the street singin' 'I Aint Got No Home'. A trip to the White House in the middle of the night with an odd secret service agent.

It all goes into the songs.

(DE):

Once I steered west with a gal that taught me films in the clogged hillbilly humidity of southern Illinois, near rivers joining below the elbow of Cairo's ghost shipyards, where Gen. Grant first steeped himself in plans to raze the Confederacy.

We burrowed past the Midwest slopes in a cramped daze, finally to settle into the West's open gut. We decided to eat in a flat, quiet park along a small river, only to stumble on a sign in official jargon and décor -- a site where Arapahoe women and children were driven down into the dust by frothing horses, cocked pistols and wool coat men.

I stumble upon these everywhere, it seems: in New York, where nothing is left of a native village but a view of a nondescript winery and a lake trembling in dust-flecked wind. The mounds of temples right off Natchez Trace, clogged with mosquitoes -- bitter fidgety swooping tiny herds gnawing at my face as I climbed past the redneck kids trying to fix a Trans-Am tire. A mound big enough to hold the bulk of a small skyscraper,
to fill with football crowds aching for touchdown bombs with faces painted like fake demented Indians torn from the back of bubblegum wrappers circa 1952.

I always thought of Oppenheimer in New Mexico, in the autoclave days, the mesquite muffled nights. Oppenheimer reading the blast as a kind of prophecy and burden, an unholy alliance with unbound machine of murder. "I am become death ... the destroyer of worlds..." Death as imminent and contained within the capsules of science, no longer landlocked, ready to be jetted into biosphere, turning cities into amber heaps, molten madness laying waste in billows of blast.

Julie and I wandered downtown Dresden, never letting Vonnegut slip far from us.
The carpet bomb inferno nowhere to be found in the recreated city panorama, just an acrid taste on the mouth of elders, or infused into

43

museum annals, juxtaposed with the rest of Plexiglass objects. Gray East German new towns gazing at us across the flat river.

What will we say of the carpet bomb of Manifest Destiny, of musty hairy disease-thronged Europe scything through the new/old land, made officialspeak by later governments in the name of democracy and progress. Progress like Salem Witchcraft Trials. Progress like slavery pushed to the borders. Progress in the name of Oppenheimer nuking the sand-sizzled southwest as Indians later mined the radioactive pits and lizards with five mutant legs skittered on cacti limbs.

I ran into a gas station on the reservation 1993. Cruising 200 down miles of trailer parks and one road, blighted -- folklore paint job clinics with bullet proof glass, Navajo cowboys talking on gas station snow-shuddered steps as pow wow music blared and people grabbed milk cartons. I stood there at the counter for ten to fifteen minutes, silent and bewildered, trying to get gas money punched into machine. No one helped me, or even looked at me. The radio heralded veterans of war, I tried not to feel ignored. My wife grew nervous in the car, unwelcome in the midnight hour. We finally made it to ice-clasped gorge with barely enough time to stick our head into the red canyon.

This land is our land, this land is your land, made for you and .... me?

South of Galveston I stumbled on the very beach footprint of Cabeza De Vaca, or so the marker insisted. He became a slave to the wetland natives, starving hysterical naked, later to become a healer driven to Mexico's inner miles. What land did he imagine underfoot? Did he foresee the Woody Guthrie dust bowel ballads, or did he believe he walked in Jesus' gait?

Buddhism is no more tired than the truths people pin on it like a donkey game for bow-legged five year olds. The claims of Christians pour down, like rhetoric aimed at control. Do this, believe this, you shall be free, but Jesus was no more free than Job, was he?

Fake politics, fake bands, corporate politics, corporate bland, feeding frenzy, buy the stocks, eat the brand, go offer your guts in the YouTube cram, not enough money for rent, no leg on which to stand, bite on the Walmart can, and make sure to devour bran, from the caucus of capitalism, to the tainted religio-autocracy of Iran, from the corolla of Canada's slightly liberal luck, to the hacks trying to make a buck.

This land is your land, this land is the next Indian Hill Rest Area, not far from the Joe Hill Rest Area, unnoticed except in the minds of leftists, aching like the band from Rockford playing his funeral processions in Chicago's meat grinder streets...

Can we create the truck stop that delivers not tepid prepackaged egg sandwiches and 500 calorie cakes but the tackle shop of truth ... not vendors of vice and planters of poison but a new network that once glinted in Ferlinghetti's eye... can we build the new nation in the hull of the old, or tear back the layers of second skin to restart Whitman's Ten Point Plan for Renewal? Can we adhere to the dream?

Gimme Thomas Paine, not pain. Not panes of corporate skyscrapers dead to the moon.

(PC): THE RUB It's great to be home. For a day or two, then the ceiling starts to drop on me. I don't want that to happen this time, and, like the fabulous visionary 60's rambler Marshall McLuhan used to say: "Nothing is inevitable as long as there is a willingness to contemplate what's happening."

What's happening, brother?

Home is the place you can't see. It's invisible, 'cause the pigment gets sucked out first, by this devouring idiot brain, me on automatic, that just wants what the bird in me wants, the animal, sex and seed, water and safety, laughs and chucklefucks. Ding dong consciousness: good/bad, sweet/uptight, up/upper, not now/later: also known as 'nada'.

Then the other people with their problems, and their problems with your problems. I call it THE RUB. "Hey what'cha doin' Peter? How come you just sittin' there staring out the window? Why don't you go mow the garage? or wash the dog, he's getting dirty layin' there in the driveway.' That's one type of homestyle torture (not one I suffer from currently, but I've been there.) THE RUB can be psychosexual dramas played out in the kitchen, the bedroom, or in front of the tube. It don't matter, THE RUB can rub anywhere in the house, there's no indoor escape. And it drains you of the all important WILL TO LIVE.

In some cultures, to avoid THE RUB, the men stand out front on the street together and smoke, all the time they're home, except for when they're eating dinner or sleeping. It's a choice I understand: get out in the coolish air, under the stars and city sky glow, looking up and down the street continually as if something's about to happen, saying off color things to the guys that wouldn't go down well in the parlor, having a couple laughs. I get it, but you can't get much done out there after a while. It can get old. It's no fun in the rain. And THE RUB is still waiting for you inside the house, it hasn't gone away.

THE RUB: stems from abuse taken at the hands of an uncaring world, years ago. It could have been childhood punishments, fatherly canings, or strange attitudes learned from the local Punch and Judy show. It could even just be genetic angst passed down on the DNA wire from the Paleolithic Era to your living room. A run-in your ancestor had with an angry gorilla or tiger... whatever the source, the ol' 'fight or flight' surfaces over breakfast comments, after lunch, or while attempting to program the tv, your IQ drops like a Jumbojet, and you're in the ooze.

I can't stand it, the pain generated in me by normal household behaviors. As a result, I was what they call 'homeless' by the age of 18, wandering the streets of a Western city, sleeping in abandoned cars, enjoying life on my own terms, I guess you could say.
I wrote a song about the other side of the homeless situation, how it was an answer for some. The song is called 'Green Blanket No. 1' and it's on the album called Full Service, No Waiting. The beauty of dawn on the empty streets, seen with the clarity of a very cold person, told in microscopic detail. I'm not trying to rationalize the pain of being homeless, or of seeing others that are homeless, I'm expressing some truth about it.

The 'HOMED' need your love too! Let's not forget about them: the people turned off and shut up by situations beyond their control, living amongst insanity day to day, hanging on for...tomorrow. A tomorrow of relief, a break in the chain, a hole in the universe, the arrival of the SEVENTH CALVARY OF THE SOUL?

a few lines (for rupert murdoch)

oh it's not funny
that pie in the face
he only has to shrug
turn away, sticking to the
lies.

publish this
you fucking killer
destroyer of the bit that's left:
drop dead.

your wealth
is a pollutant
your breath

is a poison gas
ruining everything
your face is now
a catcher's mitt

you sit there
in judgment of
mankind but it's
all over, boss,
some of these days.

(DE)

The Ramones, The Nerves, 1977…

I feel odd, being the baby brother to all that night prowlin,'
rock'n'roll hollerin,' off-the-cuff visions in America still fueled (tho
now in Guitar Hero fantasy wish fulfillment) in part by Kerouac's
dream of asphalt all-night kicks...

But now the roads are sideswiped by immense commerce and box
stores, baseball diamonds and park benches are paid for by corporate
schemes in the heartland, even in the swagger of cosmopolitan
metropolis midnights.

Being a kid brother when the Ramones and Nerves hit Poison Apple
on the highway a stone's throw from my cookie cutter ranch house,
where Michael and Laura picked rocks from the old farmland, so
Dad could plant the veldt green oasis he dreamed of years earlier in
the Missouri trailer park, where grandpa held court.

You unrolled the songs in tense hectic two minute rock'n'roll haikus, compressed history of Chuck Berry and girlpop and the Kinks coil maybe, some new kind of punk thing still in genesis stage, being born on the spot, the Ramones waiting to point the van down the flat gray highway to the next gig where kids would tear holes in their jeans to become Joey's fabled army.

I prepped for school down at Ralston, the humdrum redbrick asylum of boredom, where I studied guns from World War II at the library and devoured the Hardy Boys and monster matinees from mock-macabre television host Son of Svengoolie's outer reach.

Teachers yelled at me for cutting chunks out of my hair instead of making the clay turn into fine forms. Teachers yelled at me for kissing the cheek of a girl, sideswiping her with the slight skin of Aphrodite. Teachers yelled at me for not saying the pledge of allegiance in 4th grade, standing in the corner, smelling the old paint and winter muck.

A bald teacher sent kids into the one-acre nature conservatory, where the bees bumbled, kids dashed and darted, and he attempted to induce us into transcendental meditation as others played rough'n'ready football.

I thank all those teachers who yelled, who tried to pry us apart long enough for a tiny vision Xeroxed from Thoreau's pond, those who let me pen the biography of Johnny Rotten, because anger is an energy that became my engine of ingenuity.

I sent the Rotten collage to my brother, who placed it on the old refrigerator in Chicago's sour side, where bums pissed in his window during the night, pooling like petrol in the kitchen.

He put me in punk clothes, guided me unharmed through Cabrini Green on a bus as Bauhaus housing project hallways ricocheted with gunfire. We wound up in Grant Park, fountains dark and mysterious as huge spiders.

I painted for the first time in his dank front basement room, terrible jolted messes, heap-mounds of smelly paint. Mom sent along Dinty Moore Beef Stew; he heated it on the clanky stove, in the can. I read chapter after chapter of <i>The Once and Future King</i> at the table, as the others went dead sleepy.

In the car, a homemade tape of <i>London Calling</i> whirled as my sister drove us to ice cream on the waterfront. After she left, I stayed one more night, wanting my brother to fill the void in my life, the brother who tumbled out of the house when I was nine, only to return with peroxide hair and smoke-fouled hand gripping punk LPs.

Punk rock came to me like secret language of the living, a truth tonic, like a soothsayer in tangled two chords, like a golden oldie tune dynamited, like a bold endless rush of saccharine, like a new skin, inviting me in, like a creed and ethos waiting for me to figure them out.

It was the only door that opened and didn't feature the band director's wormy eye, the softball coach's beer belly, the basketball coach's insurance schtick, or the teachers' limp lessons.

It held me like a baby brother, ready for the wolves...

I was bitten, I was bugged, I was kicking back at the slack. The music fused into my spleen. The true escape and redemption burst just a beat away. Later, on the drum kit I could pummel the nervous system of the state, one slender splintered stick at a time.

I wish I could sell Marshall McCluhan by the pound at the local grocery store, down in the overlit aisles, next to shrinkwrapped Green Giant tomatoes at Target, where the red dot sees everything.

Got a bum leg of love, got jilted by the economic infrastructure of American laissez faire spending sprees, got jobless paranoia, got erection problems, got two kids and no future but in paradise of low-end luxury, take some McCluhan man.

If they snuck up to me to figure the McCluhan produce, I'd lean in their ear, a bit musty and kink-haired, whispering down deep, "Get yr fix now. No more cute-rate discounts. No more bird-brain. No more robot life. Think. Dispel. Decontrol."

Undo those backward flights into backwash memories meant to keep you fixated on then when now is screaming.

We cruised the dirty backside of Galveston yesterday, where the boat welders boil in the heat next to the flat gray-green water, where the quarry rocks mumble. The Ruts played "Babylon's Burning" in the CD player, storks massed and dove into water warm as a bath tub, plumbers and painters disappeared behind Victorian fences, and stores sold us cupcakes with five inches of frosting, heavy and white as a softball.

We pulled up next to a daycare I thought was empty: crusty paint, homemade all around, faded bright colors, storefront blues. Starting to aim my camera at the naive art that constituted their signage, I saw the kids pressed against the lower window dusty panes, eyeballing me with mistaken glee. Was I their displaced daddy?

This is where the kids go ... this is where the day ends, in the heatstroke draft coming in from the gulf, in the shadow of smeared doors.

The island that has no record stores. The island where Ramblin' Jack still hits the club where the roaches spin from underneath tacked faded flyers, drunk on old glue. Where the B-52s turn the rebuilt Opera House into a love shack, into a private Idaho, into a new wave volcano, even as hurricane emptied stores lurk.

As a kid, instead of Punch and Judy, I had Davey and Goliath, 6 a.m. every Saturday morning, free by myself in front of the TV, don't bother me. I gotta feel normal for half an hour, after all-night insomnia, sleeping in the shag-carpeted hallway, petrified of the cicada buzzing on window and the gong of tall wooden clock.

Leave me alone. I'd head to the backyard, fake Civil War gun ready and willing in my hands, ready for dirt bike stretches of beaten patches of forest. Big holes where the one-eyed freaks supposedly lived, next to the field of clover, next to the pits where we buried torn fragments of porn, next to drainage pipes where we melted our action figures with WD-40 blazes, where we watched the broken hearted man scurry down the gravel in his pissed-off car, hit a ditch, and propel in the air like a dying two ton beetle.

The Great Dane across the street, snapping at my mutt of a dog, scurrying, yanking the iron pole outta the ground in fury. The dead guy in the garage across the street, gas curlicuing around his limp body. The neighbor dad holding off cops with a hunting rifle, kids fleeing across our backyard. The hot air balloon catapulting to the ground behind mom and dad's garden, where they tried to grow Georgia peanuts and corn, misshapen carrots and beans.

Where the transformer blew up in a humungous cough, the dog ditched under the bent fenceline, and I stared at the neighbor's bikini. Playing Run DMC on the green chunk of furniture with the plastic LP player: "It's like that, and that's the way it is..."

Home is where the Green Hornet comic is, where the older girl takes me into the closet, hair dry and itchy in my face, rubbing me like a rag doll with puffed up parts.

Where I furtively audiotape mom and dad's parties from behind the couch. Where I shove Bibles beneath my bed as my brother undergoes treatment and my mom cries next to the washing machine, tears mashed up on concrete.

Childhood. Rock'n'roll. Nickels falling into the jukebox purchased from the Beloit College fraternity. Dad's propped it into the corner.

"I Can't Get No ... Satisfaction."

Home is where I suck on Coke bottles, where I find my dad's photocopied articles about the death of grandma.

Where I let Bob Dylan drain me, where DOA tells me "No god no state no lies..."

Don't treat me like a dead butterfly.

Gimme gimmee shock treatment.

My brother buys the album at the dust-strewn house, where the man with a million skin tags works the desk.

I am cutting up my toys with a machete.

The Dead Kennedys pound my head.

Childhood.

I am leaving you.

I have left you.

Look at me.

(PC) "Yeah or take some Burroughs or some DOA, some Dead Kennedys, man that shit straighten out your rod fix your leg a lot better than McLuhan, who after all is just asking you to THINK about what's happening..."

"Take some McLuhan man" here and the graveyard eyes and punk rock society as victim, why not "take some DKs some Ramones that'll straighten you right out man, shit look what it did for all those Orange County kids" you could whisper some Blake to the two-kids-and-no-future man, how about some Patti Smith? None of it helps if the idea is that the inevitability is all, laissez-faire sprees have taken everything, yr fucked.

No future is a state of mind, not an objective fact for anyone, no matter how sorry they or you are. There's no situation that's so bad it can't be turned around on some major level.

You 'lean over all musty and kink haired' hey bet McLuhan never smelled like that...

"Get yr future now. No more cute-rate discounts. No more bird-brain. No more robot idles. Think. Dispel. Decontrol. Undo those childhood punishments, those guy chats with venal or vexing underpinnings. Those backward flights into backwash memories meant to keep you fixated on then when now is screaming."

Yeah.

That would really be something, like psychoanalysis, the stuff Burroughs was trying to teach Ginsberg and Kerouac about. Maybe they will sell that in grocery stores soon, but I doubt it, they just give you a pill.

"There is no inevitability as long as there is a willingness to contemplate what's happening."

"You got a dome: use it." -Buckminster Fuller to George Russell

home

home is where the confusion reigns
home is where my father mops the floor with me for asking 'why?'
home is where 'I can still kick your ass' meets 'take another step and
I'll bash your fucking head in'

a kid on the corner pulled a knife on me I bashed his face in a month
or so later
two brothers who lived near the corner chased me down and beat the
crap out of me in the snow
I had crossed the street diagonally in front of their house they said I
was 'crossing the red of the duck'
the duck was me they said... the red was my blood.

home is the horrors of the local high school
    swimming bare ass naked with a hundred other boys at 8 am on a
winter's morning
    in front of Viet Nam vet gym teachers who
    hit us with rulers 'bend over and crack a smile'

home where just walking across town on an autumn night was
risking a beating from cruising 'fraternity brothers'
    as the gangs of Buffalo were called. A 'fraternity' was busted with
machine guns and a bazooka up in the local park.

home is where confusion reigns
    and I got down on my knees and begged my poor parents for help
from my madness 'til I realized there wasn't gonna be no help
and immediately I stopped crying.

home terrified to go to the big school afraid I was gonna get stomped
well I did get stomped but it wasn't so bad and THAT was a life
lesson

home I moved out the cops used to shake me down they wanted to
get me
home being called 'queer' everyday by passing car assholes etc for
my long hair
home on the highway, man, for years and years.

55

home two doors down World War I vet Howard lived drank a case
of beer a day
his brother Lee a bookie drove Cadillac and I'd go hang with
Howard
he'd always hear my mother calling

home me and my best friend one night jumped by a mob of guys
who made us fight each other or they'd kick our asses
I didn't want to do it so they formed a circle around us
and screamed to start fighting I wasn't gonna hit my pal
but he caved and punched me right in the face
this scene polled on and on
I hated those kids
they hung a kid upside down
in the garage said he was a 'jew'
used to piss out of trees on us little kids
the ring leader of those turds is now a Baptist preacher somewhere,
no lie.

home is where my friends Eric, Chris, Pete, Marianne, Mike, Jim,
and Mark all committed suicide.

home is where my friend Joe shot his cousin by accident with a
loaded hunting rifle his dad left by the door
his mother went in for shock therapy I got high on pot the first time
in their home. the cousin in back paralyzed in bed. the mother blank
in the dark house
the father gone on crime business. me and Joe laughed all night
could barely breathe.
home, three doors down, is where my other friend Jesse's mother
committed suicide, and he was put in juvenile home

Joe ran away to Toronto at 12 was gone 6 months Jesse was gone a
year or more

home is where I had a window into the world, called a record player
    Bob Dylan never drained me. he was a warrior, and passed on his
energy and knowledge to anyone what wanted it

home is where my mother wept as Bobby was assassinated I woke
up to her tears
home is where she betrayed me to my father who was gonna kick my
ass again but I fled into the night
    hearing the train whistle of the westbound midnight freight and
knew I would never go back

home is where I lost my depth perception after too much lsd
years later I thought the matrix was a documentary about my teenage
mental state

home one night in the dark dark night (nights could be very dark
there no kidding and still)
4 guys from the John Birch Society came and stood across the street
in the shadows
I knew who one of them was a guy named Wilson "hey Case
c'mere"
they were on a hate mission
I was tripping   my dad was in the house tho' so I didn't want to go
back in there...
but I did and he wanted to smell my breath. something was
happening
but he didn't know what it was, and neither did I.

so I split home
moved in with 6 guys
into a green dump by the dead lake
(the lake killed by Bethlehem Steel
up around the bend
spewing smoke and filth
 a couple miles away)
had a band called Pig Nation
we played LOUD 3 chord rock & roll
when long hair got too popular
I cut off mine super short
wore old jeans
stomped around in the rain and snow
walked on the frozen lake
in a pair of big black motorcycle boots

that I got somewhere and me
and Jesse started calling ourselves
punks. this was 1970.

I had a bad local reputation
was picked up by the cops
for questioning about an
unexplained grand larceny
mothers wouldn't
let me in the yard
to hang with their grown up
offspring and I was banned
from seeing Raven by her Doctor father
guess he knew what was what

but home is where
we had our laughs
got drunk on hard cider
me and Jesse turned
all the furniture upside down
our housemates came home
and didn't appreciate it
guess they weren't young enough
angry enough fucked enough
to see the humor.

so, a little while after that
I hit the road for good.

"and you ask why I don't live here?
honey i can't believe that you don't move"
   -b. dylan 1965

(DE):

Every time Murdoch blinks, an once of his money could jet
peanut butter straight to Somalia's lips.
I could care less about the last flight of Discovery, the orbiting piece
of space LEGOS, as the borders of the world fill with pleas...

Can you see the leer of Murdoch in space?
Can we land the metal bird on his face?

(PC):

There was a reason why I was homeless: it was a big improvement.

(DE) Is laissez fare voodoo economics a wormhole? What would Burroughs say?

Storm the citadels of cell phone towers, take back the night, re-implant the imagination?

Can we make shotgun paintings from IRS forms, from the loan papers of devil dog men in corporate suits?

No future was simply a calling card, cradled in nihilism tropes. It was the ticket that exploded. But Lydon always believed in music, in the word, in the push push of music… Can we take the Ramones in pill form, or "Pills" uttered by New York Dolls with their banshee howls, cause all that glam and glitz could never cover up the American grain, the bluesy whoop ass.

Ginsberg dreamed of Walt Whitman in the supermarket, next to the watermelons and peaches, Joe Strummer grew lonely in the supermarket listening to the hi-fi in his head. *Repo Man* guffawed in the grocery store with all the generic food labels blaring white.

"Feeling 7 Up, I'm feeling 7 up, that cool refreshing feeling, crispy clear and light…"
Otto!

William Carlos Williams discovered a poem in the middle of a grocery list, tacked on the fridge.

What did Blake see in the dead industrial atmosphere descending on him?

Home is the whole map of childhood spread round the region because the car was a babysitter, the banana-seat bike was my cell phone, because my feet were flat and crooked but they took me into the woods...

where I lit trashy trees on fire near the barbed wire fence as the huffing horses tried to stomp my dog...

home where the high school counselor was yanked out his car to the tree line, beaten to a pulp, and set on fire, because he was a closet gay...

where I stole away with an AC/DC record from a trailer where Gary lived meagerly, only to have it broken over my mom's head when my sister sassed "it's about cocaine balls!" when my mother really worried about gonads...

home where the kid living near the junkyard and sandpit swimming hole cut his daddy into pieces and planted him in the backyard

home where a girl's neighbor poked her vulva under a blanket while the whole family watched *Dynasty*...

where her brothers did things I only knew from X-rated films...

home where I buried guinea pigs under the apple tree with fungus fruit

home where the poor motley tough-ass punks threw cans at the back of my head because I wore sweaters and combat boots, a sin.

home where I surged forward at the Black Flag show, needing something undefined, only to have my left ear buzz forever...

home where we headed to the Ozzy Osbourne concert in a carpeted van, smoking a twig of pot, 10 years old as the Accept drummer played barehanded like a monkey...

home where the metalheads tied me up in the basement on a metal pole, making me huff Kleenex full of mushy Miracle Whip

home where we threw rocks over the house denting random cars, shot our toys full of BBs

and sent fireworks streaming into the gutters of neighbors, because we could...

home where the neighbor kid plowed his motorcycle into a yield sign, turning his face into mashed potatoes...

home where neighbors still die in garages filled with Nissan exhaust, just last year...

where Devo and Kiss held sway, where we built rickety half-pipes and jumped the curb and broke ice with baseball bats and nailed each other's houses with menacing golf balls...

home where the snowmobile pummeled the pipe at the end of our driveway, where 1979 spat huge mounds of snow, where I fell in the basement window as my brother slept stoned...

home where I danced like a wounded goose in the driveway shooting baskets baskets baskets, use the wrist boy, shoot, like some Jim Carroll from the pancake prairie without his attitude and murky smarts, his deep-prose and chapped lipped soliloquy...

home where I sold fifth graders marijuana roaches from underneath the passenger seat of my sister's Chevy Nova stirred with David Bowie's breath on the 8-track converter...

home where the kid walked up the quarry pile and got sucked in like a vortex of sand particles from Egypt...

where I grabbed the back of Wade on the dirt bike motorcycle feeling the wind beat back my ears and the highway whir in prolonged flight...

home where the homes took away all the open land, no more yellow spiders in the corn stubble, no more warped delinquent homemade forts, no more show me your brown nipples next to the jittery dragonfly and the lingering mosquito...

home where I smoked opium out of tinfoil at the first concert I zoomed to, in the college bar in Dekalb, where we headed home blank-faced as X played on the tape player...

where I turned the glass upside down on the hashish, letting it pool the smoke in curlicues, ready for the cold embracing inhale, drowsy as the terror movie at the mall made me loose my wits...

home where my mother took me to the old palace theaters for
Bambi's last stand, where my brother set me down in front of *Jaws*...

I've never been the same...

The kids of the black hole, I ain't trying to pretend, no Penelope
Spheeris boy here, just a kid with a few scars to mend.

(PC):

Mind-thoughts

I oughta respond more thoughtfully to your letters. They are letters, aren't they?

I've been riffing and you've been riffing back and we both answer with tangents: you tell me a punk rock story and here I come with a-guy-down-the-street-comitting-suicide type thing (man, I hate suicide) (I dig Suicide, though!) It's kind of psycho, lind of cool too, not a conversation, not a competition, but some kind of neo-beat-post-post-punk echo chamber.
Or maybe it'll be a 'good read' tho' I don't see how! Who could it be for? People like us?

We can hand deliver every copy maybe.

Or maybe I should just forget the where the who the what and just rave on:

"DO YOU EVER HAVE MIND-THOUGHTS?" (I was asked this by a midwestern phys-ed major in the 90's)

-I find it hard to accept how old I am. I'm fifty fucking seven.

-imaginational power is an issue, in the world, in my head. I realized when I woke up last night and walked around in the dark. I saw the voice of the sea, I heard the drunken boat, it all was coming in on a powerful frequency. But's its 4:48 pm right now and I'm lost as a child in the big city rain.

-sex and spontaneity: the class I flunked (except for the couple times even I passed, uptight, sheesh!).

-the only time I DON'T have writer's block is when I'm writing!

--needed: some sort of REAL redemptive experience.

-my imagination is starving

-NO GOD NO STATE NO LIES is emergency room talk, but Blake had a higher formulation. Empire and the Church were included together as enemies of the Human. He recognized that the 'God' most 'Christians' worship is also known through the ages as 'Satan,' and is the sponsor of Death. Jesus was a Prophet and an ARTIST, calling all to be creators and artists, and to live lives of prophecy and imagination. Dig ?

-I dig the detail in yr last ones. "Labor well the minute particulars" says Blake, 'general good is the plea of the Scoundral Hyporite and Flatterer.

--and then the Demons of Sleep attack, pull me under.

-the isolation of my gig hits me hardest when I'm home: on the road there's a show every night. Home, obviously I'm thrown onto my lonesome resources, completely in the present. What is the battle? Where to go? Who to love?

-its easy to be on tour and not see that you are living off your past as a songwriter, singing yesterday's tunes, yes, maybe with today's performance inspiration-but I don't believe that's as big a light as the vision that create new sounds in he first place. These days people tour all year along the channels of commerce, take a month or so off the road, scribble and hum, create some new 'product' - record and go back on the road asap - but is anything really being channeled, anything deeper, more powerful, spiritual, glimpsing the drunken boat, the promised land, the grail, or just the howl ... or are the same old tired possibilities being played out again and again?

-Coltrane, Dylan, Miles, Ginsberg, etc ... heroic striving.

Furry Lewis!!! Robert Wilkins!!! Memphis Minnie! Skip James!!!

Striving! We must strive to attain our voice, to be ourselves, to overcome all this the death around us. Excelsior!

(DE):

In the end, I consider them impure hybrids, some (to steal from the Buzzcocks) with a different kind of tension, sketches of prose in letter forms, or even better, sometimes on the edge of "promes" (prose meets poetry), how one critic tagged my writing style.

In the age of hyper-mediated messages, or instant off-the-cuff clickety clack texting, I think they are organic, candid, and spontaneous, but not mere 'typing' as some older writers would dread. Hand delivering the copy is, essentially, what selling them at gigs constitutes, a look into the echo chamber, riffage, in which our identities, idioms, ideologies, and ethos are revealed in cross-hatched layers, each strand pregnant with meaning that leads to a whole picture of personhood.

As is, I think they are overly fragmented, themes running in dizzying directions, but with a little shaping and re-organizing, I think we could have 'chapters' compiled, which I can do in middle Aug-Sept, before school heats up.

But yes, stop thinking 'bout it and do it! As you scrawl, the mind's gears go and the pistons fire -- working towards perhaps the Imagist notion of 'no idea but in things' or the satori, the sudden glimpse into ordinary experience that held Kerouac by the jaw, or to quote Michael Kimmelman waxing about demised Lucian Freud:

"The real world, stripped bare, already presented unfathomable strangeness and fascination. An artistic life should exhaust itself trying to unpack it."

I always thought the most surreal things were packed in my own baggage of life, the yards I mowed, trying to be as perfect and evanescent as an Ad Reinhardt painting, the only major abstract painter of his time that started as an abstract painter (though he illustrated for New Masses) from the get-go, even as the WPA hired him and the FBI stared him down in Communist hunts.

My dad's lawn as middle-class art piece, damaged by dandelions and tornado testiness and the kids walking home from school in dirty shoes.

Mom waxing every leaf in the house, sweeping the carpeted stairs clean of imprints,
like every day was a postcard from *Homes and Garden*, everyday unreal.

Did you walk with Rimbaud down those sidewalks immersed in sea-impressions, did you glimpse Stephen Crane's urchin girl on the corner, did you feel the weight of every step as if in an oil painting...

My fave quotes from Burroughs was when he would come back from the bathroom, and tell the *Spin* reporter, in his drawl and brittle mild-mannered way, Genet just passed through me.
That Burroughs remains lodged in my cranium, not his clinical dissociation of words and phrases, but the other Burroughs: dream machines, telepathic voices, inkblots of Rorschach swirling, Titanics drowning, St. Louis hard-ons melting into the keys of the adding machine.

Even Phil Ochs, in his sometimes stodgy delivery and crooner coyisms, in his steadfast labor as imperfect medium, each as attempt to reveal a cosmology known only to his own DNA.

Or Blake the short truncated poet "The Sick Rose": the invisible worm flying in the night with its secret love: manifold meanings cocooned in sex life, amor abstractions, relationships linked to biology, flesh and flowers...

Blake's unblinking attack on London: blackened walls, grey palls, spitting prostitutes, manacled minds, chartered streets, enslaved boys, mandated marriages, church appalls...

The networks of commerce keep most artists enthralled to audiences' needs and wants, a kind of prostitution, the Chitlin Circuit with a white facelift, tho if you think of only as an infrastructure, a ways and means, a circuitry, that enables you to forge and forage from life even as if you take an hour to entertain and explore, then all can be well, if you don't hammer down the dream.

The Borders where we met has been slapped out of business by the new models of commerce, has bitten the dust next to coiffured lawns. The others are falling like Legos once perched tight. You gripping the Louvin brothers CD, ready to roll with a John Prine "Space Monkey" tune when the fellow dumped his kids on the carpet. Even those spaces are gone.

One chain store, one indie store left, for four million people. What comes after the deluge has dwindled?

Put down your books, son, and we'll talk? Or don't bother me, I need to photograph my lunch plate for Yelp.

Help, I need somebody, help...
To restore visions back into the American backbone.

(PC):

I think we should just publish this in its original 'order,' an improvisation intact.

(DE):

Like those records that used to be cut straight to vinyl in the next room...
Or live performance, bumps and all...

(PC):

Yeah of course Jesus was a rebel. I always loved that "no stone will be left standing" promise. Total absolute anger and revolution.

But the J-Man won't go in any of our boxes. He always comes busting out. "Whatever you think it's more than that."

Artist? Prophet? Rebel? Even Phil Ochs understood? That's sayin' something.
Jesus died a criminal's death at the hands of empire after teaching about forgiveness, mercy, love, those be hangin' crimes, bwa! Think about it.

Blake's poetry doesn't need the pictures. He's a vivid, mad and genius writer. Did I say something about Rimbaud? I must've lost my mind for a second there. Burroughs, hey what do I know? I've been readin' his books since I was 12, sheesh.

I feel like I know nothing.

I tired of it all today, don't have any ideas, I'm pissed, stayed up into the grey light studying a new book Ed Sanders recommended on-line about the Kennedy assassination. Yeah, it was the CIA, aided by the FBI, the mob, other haters and nasty right wing fucks. I'm tired of it, burned, sick, sick sick...

I gotta drop out of the race for a minute, recharge.

(DE):

I was riffin' on your allusion to 'drunken boat' ya mentioned. Every
time I head to Dallas, the dead weight of history hits home there...
8 mm flash of muzzle, yellowed newspaper accounts, green slopes
sidelining street, depository windows, the car wheeling back and
forth forever...
No man alone triggered Dallas... but as me and Julie talked shop at
dinner yesterday,
L Johnson got Civil Rights passed, despite his toilet tirades...

Did he actually believe in Vietnam's build-up, where my uncle's last
stand was, discharged for being gay in 1961, part of the 3rd RRU,
the frontline grassy fields spies hunting for Viet Cong radio bursts...

Or was it the price he paid for Civil Rights, to satisfy the bile-filled
stomach of the military industrial complex?

(PC):

    blank

1:23 AM

I'm stuck. When did this day leave me here? I'm irritated. By what? My feet hurt. So what? I'm nervous. THE RUB is rubbing. I stop sentences and cross out words. Lost. Can't hear myself. Or feel my heart. This happens again, always. I'm closing down. Bugged. I got home Monday night, it's Friday now, and I'm shot. My hands are failing. I can't really type. But my heart, my head. I can't master enough belief to get through an idea. The first thing you need to write a song is the belief that you can write a song. I don't have it. For some reason, I'm out, barren, lost, shut down. It's a feeling that has me wrapped up from head to toe. Everybody comes at me with advice, its all true, but it's just bs. Nothing anybody says helps. It's my disease. I've always had it. I'm having an attack, it will pass, after I waste another shitload of time. It comes, fucks me, then leaves. I've lost my way, again.

Phranc was having a party we went over there. I could look people in the eye, even talk a little, mumbled attempts at humor, but I was hollow as an old rotten log. In Washington everything is tied up in a fuckin' mess. here I have a lot to be thankful for, a great gig just came in, a pretty swell album review in something, a lot of things are going my way. I'm workin' on this writing with you. But I've got a block in my head.

Why didn't I ever go sit quietly somewhere today, and listen? That might've helped. That's what I wanted to do, but instead I did the opposite. Ran around meaningless and dumb. I saw my friend Jerry and we stood on a streetcorner in the sun, and talked about jazz. Jerry's an artist from San Francisco and LA, via South Dakota. In 1959 or so, he met a teenager named Bob Dylan and drove all around Sioux City with him for a day or two. Bob liked Jerry's girlfriend. Jerry was into jazz back then, and Bob kept asking: "got any folk records?" When Jerry was stationed near Flagstaff with the army, early 60's, he'd go to wild parties at Robert Creeley's place. He used to watch Miles and Monk play in clubs, hung out in SF at the Fillmore. Now he's a composer and painter. We talk whenever I see him, always about jazz, only jazz. He says he's gonna bring over some George Russell records… wow. So all that was pretty cool. I was relaxed, didn't have a problem.

I go home and I get it: It's the writing!!!! Arghhhhhhh!!!!!!!

The day feels wasted 'cause I didn't get the thing I'm feeling down. Didn't get anything down. Carried it around in the heat while I evaporated.

Tomorrow.

(DE):

Walked last night down through the gray heat walls, a kind of ozone paintscape that could be sliced with butter knife, the city protoplasm thick and tangible, fogged by car exhaust, to the bookstore, seeing the people line-up with book mounds dangling in their fidgety hands, getting 10 cent discount before the whole store is scuffled, disappearing into the annals of foreclosure, just another blip on the changing "economics of scale."

Literature no more than pure weight of commerce, bad commerce that can't pay bills.
People ruffling and piling, hmming and hawing, pushing and groping, until the deep PM, the car parking lot clogged in circus mayhem. My book comes out the month that the second largest chain bites the dust. My magazine came out in the last few years before Tower Records fell off the map. I'm the guy still building Roman statues in the hinterlands after the hordes have flung themselves against the city walls.

The staunch proud right-wing act like petulant children in the White House. the *NY Times* urges the President to act like Lincoln, to act like Roosevelt, damn it, do something, be ... Presidential. The right-wing in Norway mimics the terror of homegrown U.S., using nothing more than fertilizer and an automatic gun to eradicate a generation of labor youth. The hallowed halls of 'power' in the grayest capitol on earth turn into a mile of debris, tourists speckled with glass shards and blood rivulets, since the powerful were already AWOL, out for leisure.

When will we jumpstart the travel TV show for justice, for tender mercies, for kill the hate, and let love sort it out.

Instead, we zone out, eyes wide open, flicking between Missouri truck stops, swamp critters, ice truckers, fishing frozen seas, this old house, flip your house, weird food, big food, ghost house, hoarders, prepubescent beauty queens, wedding dress snafus, the gamut of media here today gone tomorrow.

73

In ten years, will we flip through the lost episodes, trying to figure out the calculus of our desires?

The militants in Sudan deny a million dying on their doorstep. The children skinny as bird's legs, tho peanut butter packets could save them in the dust of death.

Heat wave hitting New Jersey at 108, raging in oven-like suffocation across the Midwest, Dust Bowl 1932 hot, eradicating every trace of water. Petrified forests at our doorstep, parched deer and hawks linger in confusion.

I feel as if I am in the middle of Ginsberg's footstep, nothing has really altered...

Instead of shooting beyond the moon, we put a cramped metallic miniature La Quinta in orbit, and expected U.S. children to dream, even as their umbilical chords sucked in the sounds of iPhones, their own inner space became much more compelling.

We want them to buy music when T-shirts fit much better...

They don't care about gay marriage, unless damaged by church harangues, they care about the sound of credit cards clicking.

God made us free, money made us mad.

Don't you worry, I am 85% disease free, and so is my iPad.

Years ago, stumbling through the adobe masquerade of Santa Fe, in the snake-bitten dust strewn high altitude where Hollywood actors got drunk in the crooked streets, I became obsessed with Kenneth Patchen ...who the hell even knows him anymore, his inky illustrations of animals, his painfully perfect poems:

"I am the worldcrier, and this is
my dangerous career...
The mountain is man.
Save the mountain."
He seems to resemble the life-affirmations of William Blake, the

muscular everyday phraseology of Walt Whitman, and the tone and rhythm of Langston Hughes to develop an oral-closeness in his work, to speak directly in the ear of readers, straight tonic and emergency session.

He exudes both vision and immediacy, some may slander his sentiments and proclamations, all full-throated, bounded to saving man, nature, and the sanity of things when forces try to render it all asunder. He combines candor and personality with mapping the tumult of the times, forging a staunch blend of anarchism and pacifism, and he led New Directions to sniff Dylan Thomas and Henry Miller.

In the middle of mechanized war and nuke annihilation, he drew, riffed jazz-poems, avoided giving in to the anxiety and dislocation of the era, seeing in American poetry the future that would be the beats, open-field, and New York Schools. After him came the spinning webs of new forms, new anatomies, to rob a phrase from Hart Crane.

Commit to art, to public voice, to steady unflinching gaze, to breaking the bones of isolation.

No needs for vendettas, for coercing people to get it. You gotta believe the ugliness can be at least postponed, that the savage scars can be sewn up, even healed. You gotta believe that the mountain can be saved.

(PC) I love Kenneth Patchen's poetry, started reading him as a teen. I dig the illuminated poetry he wrote, and the Journal of *Albion Moonlight* too. Yes he's a great one, his words a powerful disturbing beautiful companion. I have a record of him reading with a jazz group: "wait, wait, wait... now!'" I gave his *'Collected Poems'* to Josh when J was about 15.

Bottomlessness.

I just had a fantasy that the Republicans impeached the President with the help of the Supreme Court, over some bs, and I went out and got in my Ford and got on the highway to DC, telling my son, "wanna come? I'm gonna go die on the streets." Then I wondered if I should take a football helmet, and who else would be there.

Is the presidency, or anything else in Washington worth dying for, at this point?

I dunno. Denise is gone out, I got all the doors open, it's clammy hot in here, Rahsaan Roland Kirk is loud on the phonograph, Rip Rig and Panic. Sirens honks explosions Elvin Jones etc. I just read about singer Amy Winehouse's death. The report on Norway murders, culture death, etc.

"God made us free, money made us mad."

Yeah it's all about the bread and we're all poisoned, even old treason spraying right wing Ezra Pound would be a lefty on today's scale, 'cause he opposed usury, and that's what it's all about here. I dug some of his writng, but man he was confused, tho' he apologized, recanted his "stupid suburban anti-semitism" to Ginsberg, (see 'Composed On The Tongue')

What is money but an imagined antidote to FEAR, it's all about the FEAR: of the bottom, of violence, disease, bogeymen, immigrants, FEAR of sex, and of people with different sexual orientations, FEAR of being broke and adrift in a cruel world, FEAR of our own cruelty, FEAR of our selves and our minds, our hatreds clung to like life rafts in a boiling sea, FEAR of cancers that drain the bank account, even the super rich don't have enough money to buy off DEATH forever!

It's causing panic. DEATH! FEAR! "don't ask me to pay for anyone elses poverty, I may look rich, but I can't afford the payoffs myself!" "I can't buy off my own DEATH!"

America corrupted by fear and materialism, no faith, no true ghosts, just Stephen King's cartoons, no true magic, just special effects.

If you can't walk through walls, the walls will walk through you! FEAR! DEATH! HELP! POLICE! LIFE ITSELF IS TERRORIZING ME!

No life without death, folks. If you can't help the poor you'll never have enough money. If you don't stop and take a breath and quit running around like a crazed fuck, you'll never, ever, have enough time. If your prisons are hell on earth, you will never be free. If you fill your rooms with the rubbish you buy, there's no room for YOU! Or anyone else!
FREEDOM? Freedom is what you CAN do. Forgiveness.
Acceptance of eventual worldly death, now. You CAN see the poor, spread the wealth, now. Life is possible, but it's not guaranteed. No party of squares can ever set the people free. Your feeling won't kill you. Take a ride DOWN, baby. Touch your feet on the bottom! You'll find your fears are bottomless, and so is everything else.

(DE):

Poems hit me at the back of my head in Wal-mart dull and insistent, in the florescent jumble that sanctions a lack of clothing for the curvy ones...

Poems hit me like still irksome charcoal at the car lot, where the heat cascaded off hoods and wheel caps, and the guy smiled like a Cheshire cat. Poems hit me in the face, full frontal muzzle of meaning, on the highway, 80 mph, nowhere to go but home, where the roaches danced macabre in my kitchen last night, choking from cans of chemicals I can't pronounce.

What path has led us to this place, to the death of a singer in her 20s frail and faulty, ready to grip down and awaken on the mic with Tony Bennett beside her, only to stumble like some YouTube Greek tragedy, a sudden turn of fate that devours mercilessly. Her voice digitized for the catatonic masses needing their fix of her failure.

What path has led us to the children shot down on rocks and gray ripples and tree limbs and caves and bushes to the sound of a gun's horrid arithmetic. The slaughter of innocents was never so easy.

Disabled children dumped in a store entranceway, shoved in the cart like last week's frozen dinners. The children stumbling under the bridge as mom pushed through the titanic heat, until a fancy fashion shoe fell off. Momma cussed, and the whole gray corridor shuddered.

I wish I could take you to see the FEMA trailers, lined up near the interstate overpass, the dead rhetoric of help, the formaldehyde of sorrow.

The apartment complex down the block, overgrown, looted, car parts piled up like rusted intestines, and wooden barriers peeled away -- HUD housing once meant to pave the path of future success.

No more than a welt of brick and masonry and chunks.

"O generation of the thoroughly smug and thoroughly

78

uncomfortable," penned Pound, who surmised that the "filthy, sturdy, unkillable infants of the very poor ... shall inherit the earth."

What will they do with the steering wheel?

Will they join Pound in his rant against "unamiable liars, bog of stupidities, usurers squeezing crab-lice ... arse belching preachers ... obstructors of knowledge, obstructors of distribution."

All the userers that maim the stone cutters, tear the hearts from lovers, make the instruments go blunt, that make the grain anemic, that turn lovely stones to cancer, that cut off the life of children in womb...

Or will they put Pound back in the fence-box, under the all-night army glares, his frothy radio voice too much to bear, his politics too impatient and outright duped by fascism's myth...

Or will they make bread with Pound, who announced the death of the old institutions…

Is he now the pig-headed father with whom they will make the compact, carve the new wood, and begin the commerce?

The Final Adventures Of The Plane That Never Flies

There is a plane warming up its jets on the tarmac. It's long and white and the windows are all blacked out. It is the Plane That Never Flies. Late at night it pushes back from the gate and heads out on its mysterious errands, taxiing down a back runway to the other end of the airport, passing out through a concealed gate and taking to the streets of our states. Once it gets out in the city, it takes on the appearance of an old dumpy off-green ice cream truck. There's a little song that plays, but don't be fooled. It's really movin'...

No one knows where it goes, why it goes, or even when. No one sees it return, yet in the morning, there it is again, parked at the usual gate, silently waiting for a pilot, passengers, directions, fuel. The air whistles through a hole in the hold– a stream of many colored waters pours out of its wounded side. The window is cracked only to reveal another cracked window beneath it. This is the only true story of its last flight: or shall we say: The Final Flight Of The Plane That Never Flies.

It wasn't a flight at all, and you and I are the only ones who know. The others look and walk by, as if they've seen nothing. That's the way it is these days. It's dead around here.

Liquor is the motor for people slow to drop. Confession is the logical extension of knowledge, but guilt is the answer to paradise. The PTNF is on a waterless landing pattern, blessed by the Scotch-Hop General and radically insane: search for the missing Nation and destroy it in its Nowhere-ness with Nothing Blasts.

Marshall this you drum-tap fools: you can cook my jaw!

The Plane That Never Flies (pt. 2)

I was husked by age

feet tied together

by invisible bolts

my look is like headlights

on a mountain road

my breath like a bad accordian

my memory is like a wet newspaper

my habits unspeakable

my imagination is a trained bird

one wing clipped

flies in circles round the house

but never breaks away

into the sunset out by the inlet

when the water flows 'til your pants are wet

and the palm trees sway in a straight line curve

makin' you wish that once you had the nerve

to get up on top open your shirt

dare all the arrows you lost in the dirt

just once take the chance and bare all the hurt

spit at the words take the long ride

let the world know what you're breeding inside

no hiding inn or retractable pen

this is the trial that you've been facing since… when?

this is the plane that never flies

its blip is pasted on my fretboard

its outline is sinking by the seaside

this is the plane that never flies

but it tells its story with head held low
all dressed down with nowhere to go
but up and out and in and then
down and out and back again.
this is the plane that never flies
but is always working on a plan.

- make me chortle/ said mayor yorty/ poems/ tied to rocks/ crash storefront windows: 'thanks for the help'/ a riot broke out/ poems were found soaked in kerosene/ two drunks were arrested/ insulting each other in sonnet form/ poetry lives/ and dies/ in the mouths of poets/ and will be sold off by the yard at the Borders garage sale/ meanwhile suicide reigns/ what used to be the suburbs/ is now called/ County Jail/ there's no room there/ for guards/ prisoners/ wardens/ cops/ or other workers of the new peace/ 'the kind of peace most people want is just another kind of war'/ pure poetry is wet/ shining/ writhing in the sun/ the stream is dry/ the poem flops on the sand/ gasping/ while the football team reaches in to their plackets and fishes out their cocks/ to take a good long piss/ poetry/ always refreshes.

-disaster movie "who's flying this plane?'/ "me sir" said the little tyke from down the street/ straight into the mountain side/ cascades of orange and blue green flame followed by sudden dismemberment/ no one's idea of/ a hot night out with the girls/ they used to make it up, life/ now it's laid in like old tuna fish/ out front they've posted a guard/ dirt yard drugs and a mad dog/ immigrant dosage/cops speed past/colorful umbrellas/beach togs/ little apartments where Riley once lived the life and tightened screws for Douglas Aircraft/ a war was on/ now the war is always on/ the thousand years war/ don't worry/ you won't have to read anything/ hear anything/ see anything too challenging/ hey what's that smell?/ it's the sewers of america/ open for business.

-Maybe it was a slap across the face that did it/ could've been the assassinations on television, or the time I nearly set the house on the fire/ one of those long horrorshow Fridays when they left me alone at night as the drove to the city for fun/ maybe I was just a numbnuts for awhile/ whatever it was, I went blind/ pictures of the Beatles in a magazine 1964. My first guitar was a beautiful black sunburst/ I'd kiss and pet it for hours/ alone in my room/ stroking its long hair/ crushes on a girl in school named Cheryl Graber/ she looked at me and smiled/ but the world soon went black.

I learned to see/ in New York City/ one Friday night/ in May/
1970/ I'd just been robbed at knifepoint/ on St. Mark's Place/ it
seemed like the whole city/ was going nuts I was with a friend/
Jesse, we'd hitchhiked from Buffalo on a teenage pretense/ of him
reuniting with his estranged father/ on the Upper West Side/ Jesse
went into the building/ and I settled into a booth in the the coffee
shop/ to wait for him, a few hours/ if needs be/ they'd let you hang
out in restaurants back then/ I was gonna read the Ken Kesey book
I'd brought/ while him and his dad worked it out upstairs/ 'til it got to
the point/ where they would invite me up/ but here comes Jesse
walking into the coffeeshop/ five minutes later/ his Dad hadn't let
him in/ we were sort of shocked/ Jesse more than me/ it caught him
by surprise/ we didn't know what to think / or where we were gonna
crash/ so we headed down to the village on the subway train

He fell in with us/ "where you guys from?" he asked/ then pulled a
switch blade and held it on me/ "see those guys up on the corner?"/ I
looked up/ saw the gang staring back/ "give me all your money or
we'll murder ya"/ my travelling cash was in my boot 16 dollars /I
had a buck in my pocket/ I handed it to him/ "you gotta have more
than that man/ I know you got some money on ya"/ "no man that's
all I got"/ "don't lie to me man, we'll take you in the alley and cut yr
throat'" / "no, man that's it'"/"all right, then ok..." he said/ rolling up
his sleeve/ showing us his forearm/ "I'm sorry man, I got a habit"
/they slipped away /across the street a cop stood/ with his back to the
traffic/ watching a mob of teens/ bust out the window of a shop/ and
start looting items out of the window

I panicked/ took off down the crowded sidewalks/ walking fast as I
could/ Jesse followed me/ and right behind him another guy/ a
bearded, blackhair freak/ followed us/ "I just got ripped off, man!"
the guy said, "I just got ripped off!"/ a man was lying unconscious
on his back in the middle of the sidewalk/ I stepped around him
nearly colliding with a flower vendor/ the streets were jammed/
loud/ the light was a gas that fell like poison/ yellow brown circles
of glow/ taxistars and corpsetrucks/ the smell of the curb/ bad fish
from the fishwagon/ stealing my breath like a hollow gut punch/ A
teenage girl began following us/ she carried a backpack/ I pushed my
way through the crowd/ watching everybody from the end of the
block/ to here.

―

Wig! Mr. Brotherman Rock&Roll

-When I was nearly 3 years old/ Wig the Rock & Roll man he says
'get your mom and dad to let you stay up late for bandstand'/ he says
'hide behind the door and poop yr jeans while listening to hound
dog'/ that broke up my sister's party/ a few years later/ he advised to
'talk out jokes in class/ make everybody laugh'/ so I did/ earning
respect and face slaps from teacher/ then he told me to punch that
bully in the nose/ ecstasy as the blood streamed down with a tough
guys tears/ and his best friends turned theirs backs on him/ Wig the
Rock & Roll Man laughed/ said/ 'you're alone now kid/ you can do it
all'/ on a fishing trip in the bush/ heard Dion singin' Ruby for the
first time through a car radio/ saw his picture in the five and dime
bubble gum machine by the door. Dion sang 'when will you be
mine?/sometime' and I got it.

Next there was the used record called shut down/ and vandalism
raids on untenanted houses in the neighborhood/ One night we hid
behind the hedge with a pitcher full of ice cubes, which we threw at
the car of the Dog Killer, a so called adult/ we let him have it good
and he never knew who or what/ we ran in the summer night/ in the
provincial dark of mosquitoes and humidity a million miles away
from New York and L.A.

Wig came to see me while I was taking my Saturday bath/ said 'here
dig this cat, he'll kill ya" like a rolling stone by a guy apparently
named The Mouth/ the poison had been poured in my ear, the
porches of hearing, eruptions, then more footsteps in the darkness/
this poison whereby I can live/ the drumbeat of disengagement/
leaving the ball team/ the boy scouts/ lessons and finally school/ in
quick order/ 'the quitter'/ my poor father loved to mouth/ but I was
just getting started.

Rock & roll every morning before school/ rock & roll every
afternoon/ every daydream had a pile drive beat or else wailed like a
harmonica bum on a freight train, thank you Brotherman Wig now I
can live without working/ by walking through walls/ a thief if needs

be/ stealing what I need under cover of here comes the night b/w Gloria/ who bit me in a tender place after my last at bat/ we were strolling round the diamonds, walking the tracks/ looking for a place nobody sees/ just like you taught me Mr. W/ yes Wig my brotherman showed how to smoke pot drop pills stay up all night wandering and get home at 3 am reading about China. It didn't matter/ I quit school on his best advice/ set out on revolution with a gang of dwarves/barking like a dog/ down on all fours, beaten like a cur, too, God, how long did that last?

Forever one night/ gimme shelter on the jukebox/ rescued half past eternity by orange juice and the walls kept moving/ out in the streets/ walked out of my body/ everything looked flat like a movie screen/ soon after in downtown Buffalo chanting ' fuck the pigs' before they attacked swinging night sticks/ Wig the Rock & Roll Man was there watching as the FBI picked me up for investigation/ something about a bank/ later/ another one about some missing coins/ I knew I was innocent. Dorian was held 8 hours on a murder rap in South Dakota they pulled him off a train. Mr Rock & Roll Wig said you got nothing to cry about son dig this: but when I started running I looked down and I was on his back all the way to to San Francisco.

Wig! The King Of Rock & Roll shot craps in the alley at daylight, stole doughnuts choked at the cow palace boogie show/ chain smoking camels/ got in terratorial fistfights with knife wielding interlopers/ was arrested again/ bailed out or otherwise released but never set any more free than/ when Wig the R&R shivered/ while killers terrorized the city/ he wept to see the nerves and crime reparing flats on the shoulders of the San Leandro Freeway interchange/ swingin' a red cape at the bull/ chasing kicks in 30 cities/ sleeping on floors/ awake for the whole summer give or take a couple nights passed out in strangers beds/ Wig taught me to twist the tales/ especially to always when/ talking to myself. Thank you, Wig finally/ for some sizeable bits of truth/ that's what kept me goin' all these years.

So, now it's been six thousand years of rock & roll/ everything keeps on changing/ I wander lonesome sometimes/ like a stray boxcar/ 'Baltimore & Ohio' what's that doing out here?' But it all works out/ my people bring love/ I do too/ and something always happens/ even

---

if it's like goin' over Niagara Falls/ or puttin' out yr own single.

Oh Lordy/ that's enough of this/ Wig! shut yr pie hole/ Jesus Christ!

(DE):

Do we have to scrape the old throats like Dylan for our irreducible
revolution, or can we just stop eating our children, armed by god
with Euro rifles, bent on remembering Vienna and the Muslim
conquest, calling massacres a "market strategy" for the new nation to
wake up to...

will we push down the panic and let the children go, commingle like
Coltrane's snaky sonic shivers

why were we born into jazz jailed, or railyard blues forgotten, isn't
our American birthright to recall the quivers of Angola?

why does the populace like living iron-clad, tightwad, heavy fisted,
inundated with T-shirt politics, cheap commodity labor, single
language, American cheese ideology?

eat the lead poisoned tuna fish, force the screws on the Douglas
Aircraft, tie rocks to your feet and jump in the waste sludge bayou,
suck on the gasoline spigots...

pills make you a better football player
pills make you better mom
pills make you a better kid
pills keep your wife happy in bed

can we paint ourselves out of manacled minds, can we repossess our
brains long enough to tell some basic truths

life is essentially a form of music, staggering wild from the heart,
wanton at times, raw as the moon too, but also measured...

I want to investigate the riot in the patterns of life
the conference of the skin mucus bone

Tom Paine still tickling the skull of American words
no more broadband suffering no humane socialism with an ugly eye
on immigrants

no liberal democracy requiring the maintenance of the top 1%
no more deals with the ones that dream like demagogues

we want the seed that tears the stone, the glimpse of lives between
the lines
not a gulag masking itself as a think tank

this is the hard work worth doing

fertilize and foist new breeds

push the "stark dignity of entrance ..." as WCW said,
let the children root, grip down, awaken.

the world need not be balanced on a knifepoint

on the upper west side of lost lame fathers
on the smashed storefronts and derelict police
on the blunt achey red arm hole of addiction
on the saccharine of bubblegum machines
on the rancid fish of thieves

(PC):

Bill Morrissey RIP
"the angels laid him away..."

Bill Morrissey died
late last night
in a hotel room in Georgia
he was on a tour of the world
that no one ever said or thought
 was gonna be 'neverending'
or still the pain
he was a friend/ one of the funniest
one of the saddest one of the orniest
people also a really moving singer
 and a songwriter/ one of the best
he is one of the brothers of song

Bill sang broken heart music
drank booze he had a mad thirst
that killed him
we met on the road
in the 1980's
both of us divorced
recently and bummed
we sat up all night
in a west virginia hotel
playing every john hurt song
we knew all the same ones
just about all of them
we laughed and talked
til the sun came up

toured together in Alaska
winter/ on little airplanes
with hunters etc...
waited to get picked up outside
at the frostbound airport
in Fairbanks it was 40 below.

the Innuit lady driver told us
its goin' down tonight but assured us
"once it gets under minus 40
you really can't tell the difference"
"we know that" said Bill

killing himself with booze
shaking in the mornings
never played drunk
but after the show...
I'd been through it myself
tried to pass on
something I knew would help
but no but no but no
always a million reasons
why shit stays fucked up

the night I met him
he gave me his record
called 'standing eight'
and that's about right
except he didn't lose
on points

i'm sad
can't say enough
gonna quit right now
goodbye bill
he went on the road
alone like me
and i hate to hear of
lonesome hotel room death
i hope it wasn't too hard
but I know it must've been
oh man

broken heart singers
are your friends
on the broken heart nights
 but was someone singin' for Bill?

farewell friend
I hope to see you
on the other end of time

freedom fighter 13
The moon was giant
 only one week back/ now
 all that reflected light is
darkness/ that roams and rules
over the Big Dark while
Freedom wrings her hands
 and weeps

In Amercia
& Brutain
Over Rance and Pain
Eat-a-ry too
has many sorrows
but Noway is the
King and Queen of Got The Blues

"White people got the blues now
   let's play something else"
said Miles to Herbie

'You got a dome, use it!'
said Buckminster Fuller to Miles pal
   the great George Russell

Singers die in lonesome rooms
cheap hotels are the best revenge.
the grass is now several shades
of digital green/ screen time torture
is the new coffee klatch.
the book store is closed
   the books wait in the cold silence/
      and they're scared

Fluerette Africaine plays
   on a / beat up phonograph near you

the Pan Afrikan People"s Arkestra
   celebrates 50 years can you see 50 more?
a woman plays the flute like molten silver
   then sings/ sheets of sound/ clear as rain
free admission and empty seats
but while we were diggin' the music
   the dancers were soulfully estranged
 and even after 50/ "the great Horace Tapscott
     is not for sale."

Believe it.

What difference to us/ if the markets crash?
   people/ already out of work/ can't lose a job
    they ain't got.
health care? it ain't for everybody/ anymore
 they tryin' to take us down:
 for people like us/ not sucking on the corporate tits
it's endangered species day:
   -"it's hard to be a free lance poet" t-bone warned me
   way back in 1n 1985. (one of us must know!)
sheesh! it's hard to be anyone now/ or anywhere at all
and if you ain't got Mr.Bill footin' the medical
   and tax right off the cliff car rental pocket
charge for finger fuck then try it you'll like
to be number two again after all that fresh air
you got it coming
and I'm lovin' it.

Belly achin baby-dolls
    in ti-chi underwear
 notice how madagascar nascar
  is never called the next big thing
but also dig how no one talks ever
about the NBT anymore/ 'cause the next big thing
    is a boom!
the soul juice dna/ as applied to upper broadway
  is dried and caked
on the stock exchange floor
   no more big things/ sorry

PAC-MAN ate the World Trade Center
  Tower Records and Lauren Bacall

The Sex Pistols came for Mountain Dew
The Beatles for Rolaids
Dylan for Stockings Panties & Bras
Highway 10 is backed up
   from LA to Tejas and back again
jammed in both directions
   air hot as
 an atom blast
blink yr eyes and ask:
justice is a word
and words are turds when used by birds
blinded by beaks/and then you hurd:

"market solutions" are code for government clampdowns
"freedom" is code for profitable military entanglements
"freedom fighters" aka corporate mercenaries are
"protecting our country" NEWSPEAK for war against
      third world poor/ half way around the globe from America
"entitlements' are what you paid for that they don't want you to have
      when you are old or sick.
(and by 'they' I mean the corporate rich)
In Europe 'entitlements' are known as 'the safety net.'
etc..
the fog of electric breath
   disaster news/ I want to shrug
off/global village bringdowns
Vikings murdering people that's new
   if you don't count Leif Ericson
We've been doing it for centuries
Right Wing hate Beasts grow and flow
  and who's gonna take it on?
Horrors, terrors, nightmares
the new moveable feast
coming to your neighborhood soon.

Big Beat signal obsession/fascist grooves
   hip hop hard of hearing/ who's doing

———
94

the heavy lifting for heavy metal these days?
It's so light it crumbles and blows
The punks are unks/ old men gettin' off of
junk/ still not as old as yesterdays styles/ yesterdays trash
on yesterdays piles still havin' a bash.

It's gettin' to be bye bye time
who can you talk like, Alphonse?
you made the wall of marble but
    we don't need your hall of fame:
we need education.

Hot New Series!

Bus was smashing the panes out with a toy hammer, as a little girl
with a heavy coat and earflaps on watched from the stoop, and
sucked on a piece of red ice wrapped in a napkin.
Shreds and shards dusted his black shoes, a cloud rose from the
floor, the moonbeams turned green, the heat also radiated in waves
from the black macadam of the landing strip.
His guitar was propped against a caterpillar, the silver strings wore
bracelets, the sound hole laughed quietly to itself. Up on the head-
stock the guitar's big ears protruded from the side of it's combover.

"By the power invested in my by the state" Bus intoned, and took
another swing at the glass.

The door to the garage opened slowly and like a dim thought, the
railroad cop entered, one misunderstood piece at a time: first, the
peaked cap, then his brown-shirted head and shoulders, followed in
moments by the rest of his uniformed body, truncheon fastened to
belt, pepper spray, dangling, clownshoes bringing up the rear, face
like a carved pumpkin.
This is the blues no one plays no more. Bus wheeled, eyed the
peeler, grabbed his ax, and aped for the stair-steps. The cop pulled
his revolver like he was landing a big floppy fish, and fired three
shots into the little girl, blam blam ka-blam!

Another job well done by our treasury men in action, nothin' fair about it.

At this point the song takes over, and a six foot blue dog in a top hat, named Huckleberry Hound, begins to dance, wearing a mask from Haiti, and hollering the names of saints. The little flap happy child with the holes drops her ice cube and makes for the territories, stanching the blood with an old transistor radio.

But it was far too late, all the messages were out and on the floor. Bus dove off the ledge, the little girl grew up into a responsible right wing courtier, and the curtains were drawn again, on a scene straight out of Whistler.

(DE):

I

We ate hungry on the discolored carpet, legs intertwined, spooning noodles into each other's mouths.
Next to us the typewriter lingered. Smooth paper groomed the inside roller.
"How's the writing?" she asked
"It's getting there."
"It's getting where? Are you really a writer?"
I saw the backlash glint in her eye.
"It's what I know. Some guys know cars."
There was so much unsaid. How I had been addicted to
broken inhalers. The yellow high. Then cigarettes. Then sex.
"Whatever," she said, flippantly,
 "Your food's practically petrifying on the plate."
I plucked at the cauliflower with a spork.
A grin drew back her lips.
"See, now I sound like a writer."

II

"The sink's full, anymore dishes?"
"Nope," I said, putting my hip against the oven door.
"Got any sex stories?" she asked.
"What do you wanna do, pin them on the refrigerator like report cards?" I replied.
She reached over. I stopped thinking.

Her fingernails rolled under my chin, longer and longer. Then pressed them against my neck. Spots began to burn behind my eyelids.

"Stories take too much time."

(elastic briefs gray with saliva ... steam crushing bathroom mirror ... telepathic bodies ... rustle of grimy shower curtain ... thighs brushed in elongated moments ... hands move like a silent wind, leading inside ... a million florescent bulbs explode along the vertebrae)

III

The cat pushed its head between our relaxed bodies, dividing us like a lid from a threaded cylinder.
"It takes time for him to get used to people."
Her voice was enervated. The flush in her face was gone.
"Do you need me?" she asked.
I did not move my lips.
"Nevermind. Not important."
I got up, feeling my abdomen with fingers light across the nudge of my belly. The sweep of the shape felt vulnerable.

The bedroom light was on, barely. Music crept in from the floor vent. Our neighbors had a Vietnamese station cranked, but the whine of bedsprings still fell out the window.

She sat there, rolled up in a half-tangled sheet, lumping arms and elbows together, like some backlit, soft wreckage.

Something in the pit of my stomach gave way. I heard muted voices.
Almost nothing. But enough.

I couldn't shift in the tight, almost loathsome insect curl of "I need
you."
Her arms fell to the side. She was still. An absence.
A shadow sliced across her torso.

I turned off the lights, then drew up against her. She came closer,
touching me with one arm, shuddering a bit. She drew the other back
behind her head, tangled in the alarm clock cord.

By 11:00 in the morning, the humidity coiled around us. She got up,
stretching and elongating her narrow chest.

Outside, sheets drifted on the neighbor's clothesline, wrapping on
the rusted yellow poles. The tip-ends of flowers folded in on
themselves in the stifling heat.

"What are you doing today?" She asked, following me to the
kitchen.
She clasped a spoon, rolling it in nimble, baby-pink fingers.
"Work, you know."
There was no milk, so we relied on water to soak up the cereal.
"Why don't you hang out with me? I could make it good for you."
I looked around.

A chair, dilapidated and wired together. Walls fidgeting with bugs
here and there.

IV

I hiked down the nearest avenue, lulled by the rumble of the elevated
train. Veering to the left, it plunged into a black tunnel below shops
pasted with *Weekly World News*, whose headlines stared at me like
paralyzed slot machines. I moved towards them, reaching out in
reluctance and boredom.

A blank face squeaked, a claw-like hand grabbed my rumpled dollar
bills and pressed change cold and flat in my palm.

I neared the rippling river smeared with oil specks. Homeless gadgets, dead bikes, contorted pipes, brown bottles, and chewed automobiles rimmed the edge.

Men set chairs down and fished, yapping phlegmy and lackadaisical at each other's stories. Pigeons darted over their poles.

They tossed an occasional mud-slicked shoe at them. Or did nothing, chewing stubby cigarettes, waiting for the slim, deformed fish to nibble at their bait of cornflakes and liver.

I slipped into a Polish restaurant. My waitress was a pudgy, chain-smoking, badly bleached hair mother to all the immigrants and drifters, teenage good-for-nothing boys and jukebox cooks.

She served potato dumplings, crowned with sweet cooked onions. When I gave her an extra buck for the top, she smiled, letting me glimpse the silver caps lining the back of her mouth.

The light outside was crushed orange.
I stood at the F-train entrance, next to mangled iron stairs, unable to go anywhere.

Raindrops fell on the asphalt, dotting the sidewalks and evaporating in the late summer combustion of Southside Chicago.

I stood there, feeling luckless, with the greasy tang behind me.

V

This is a near-slum.
The year is 1992.
Dusk begins to fall on the bodegas
and their fly-eaten lettuce,
lottery tickets, and soup cans.
This is the clatter and clank of the train.
This is a street with no name.
A leftover sun kicks at my feet.
The night smells of gasoline and urine,

mingled with the dreams of America
that go through a door
unalarmed, shoulders slumping.

Notes Upon Listening to The Records of Lemon Jefferson
I was drawn to the traveling performers passing through. The side show performers - bluegrass singers, the black cowboy with chaps and a lariat doing rope tricks. Miss Europe, Quasimodo, the Bearded Lady, the half-man half-woman, the deformed and the bent, Atlas the Dwarf, the fire-eaters, the teachers and preachers, the blues singers."   -Bob Dylan

Dream---*Astronaut training with mad uptight instructor. He meets her and looks in her eyes and says she's 'gay' because a 'the spark he gets from women isn't there' type-thing, he has beautiful model-like girlfriend and he's the leader and the big guy on a stick, getting ready to go up in big rocket but we're on platform above swimming pool, she's with him on a platform one down and I'm above- she's nervous to dive from up here but you have to. It's my turn and I don't want to do it, and don't. He comes up and gets ready to force me, he, I'm afraid, will sabotage rocket to kill me, I'm at his mercy, he comes up and knees me and I tell him I'm freaked out and no can do. (map of beach area with planes and arrows and fake directions to throw off enemy.)*

Blind Lemon travelled through Beaumont, came to a stop by a stand of bare branch trees in a hard scrabble rocky acre of dirt and stubble, called the end ground. Emptiness and sunlight, the wind as a home for starlings and straw, whistled his last number for weariness, wickedness, evil tempers and streetcar number nine. White men lassoed by car dealerships and ladies of Scaramouche, presented in living bras and closet girdles hummed for silken fantasy whipcrack garden shacks, and waved goodbye with blood stained hankies, forlorn, fishing for complimentary pre-game hotdog joints, chambers of horror and South Congress big boys, forgotten, forgiven, for shit, f'r y'all.

I heard the jangle of his tangled moss, the sound hole gaped, the tuners turned and the strap struck the hour.

"Showtime, blindman, everybody's in."

Blind Lemon got up the neck, unbound by fools, a see through scene, and broadcast for the whole neighborhood, stricken.

Shuckin' Sugar.

Dream---*Picked up by little man from outer space and his passenger in a fast sports car, with a backseat, sort of a muscle car. I'm with Joey my songwriting buddy from A Million Miles Away and Lost Time. The little man is driving fast, insanely, it's an evil vibe, just racing for destruction. I am feigning no fear, even egging him on. Also, pretending that I'm in control and can drive the car sideways. We hit a new kind of curvy rising and falling country road. Alkes & Fradkin in a store or space...*

The people went out and waited when they heard the train coming. Some old crow barked at 'em from the telegraph line. The wind moaned, the sky, of course, was grey.

The little black train smoked in like a fat man's rod, shook and died and the crowd pounded off. Lemon was in, off before they got out, draggin' a doctor's satchel, and had a little red guitar around his neck, dangling from a string. To the children he looked like an illustration from a book, the giant friendly talking mole, little useless glasses up on his nose and a goofy laugh. To everyone else, he was invisible, just a sharp-suited city boy decked with mud, clothes slept in and on, shoe leather expressive of long wandering.

They called him a seer sucker and a navy Dodge. They manipulated his cornflakes, conned his quarters with the flick of their crooked wrists, and all he ever did was rock and roll. "Steal my money I'll go get me some more" he said and did and that's the corner of our story-Dallas 1923 Deep Ellum a blind man singin' and little boy Lightnin' collectin' the change and leading the Blind Man, Lemon, off and away, past the windows of sin.

He was blind, man, but he saw the whistle of tin, the truncheon swing, heard the flatfooted steps of the Dallas heat and read the book of darkness for all Fort Worth, now feeling his way up a sweet thing's leg, a perfumed corner in the back of a strange saloon, she with the sing-song voice and a flapper's hat, beautiful strong body in a party dress, and the smooth, tight, slippery flesh slide of the thighs towards cotton and honey where he found his bearings and took the ride while watching the door with his earlobes.

The piano player came back and kicked the tin spittoon at the end of the bar, Arlene petted his big wet head, led him to water and bid him drink. And drink he did.

Drunken spins...

His strummin' leads us and it's early Springtime, out by the bare branches and open spittle flayed fields, bitter cold like a spinsters judgment, where emptiness rings like a nickel in a bucket. Tuned down low, roll the E down to B flat, they say it's the key of the cosmos, the clouds, the constellations that watch like birds on the line, while crows shout at Crazy Lemon on his way to the train.

He feels someone is listening. He knows you're there. Eighty years can't dull the sensation or rub it out of his heart, he's a big man but he wears a skeleton around his neck, dangling from a string. Just like his heart.

They all looked up when he sang. Not that business stopped but a memory crested the bar and broke over their dizzy heads like storm surf on the Texas plain. Back then Dallas was a border town of sorts, the meeting of home hell and nowhere, and tho' Trix ain't walkin' no more, in '19 Blind Lemon wasn't a star and Robert Johnson was still a child. War broke out everyday in east Texas, and the Ku Klux Klan rode 'til dawn, whip cracking, shack burning, lynch mobbing, destroyers, killers, white men spreadin' the word of you-tell-me-who these cross boxers worshipped. It's not who they said. Years later they'd turn down Jesus for membership to the country club, but gave an okay for the sheriff's men. So many black men were murdered in Navasota, the President sent the army in, what year was that anyway? So the little children grew up in fear of a real live white boogie man, and the one following the gang, eye squint shut, that's Lemon, learning by touch the hard and soft, the smooth and wet, the feel of fungus on bark, the crawling anthills mound. Kids played tricks on him but he paid right back: Beware the blind man's masquerade, when he dons a disguise it's more than a costume ball.

2.
"You're gonna need somebody on your bond." -Blind Willie Johnson

"You gotta have somethin' to get you through, especially when they tryin' to kill ya'. I made a big sound with my voice, and when I was singing on Deep Ellum they said you could hear me three blocks away over traffic. An' I could make that guitar call your name if I wanted, I could make it howl like a dog or move like a lightnin' strike. It'd shout and sing right along with me, behind my voice like a crazy band and that's my way. Some folks said I'd lose the dancers, but I could hear 'em out there, I'd hold a hundred of 'em there, right by the 'lectric car line, gettin' somethin' to hear while they throwin' their money away. It took me a while to get but once I did I never went hungry or dry, again. Never got so lonesome as before either. Never had another problem. Well that ain't true but get what I'm at, I made a way with music. and see, I had a plan, my songs added up and people knew my name: there was a lot of good will, I could go where I wanted and get all I need, on my side of town anyhow. Sure, I played some parties for whites, they'd come and laugh and carry on and just miss the whole damn thing, but that's how they was, like they missin' their whole damn lives. And if I got too drunk around 'em they'd fetch the cops and always had a cell for me then. Up on Deep Ellum Street, some of 'em shops liked me and some had no use for it."

We don't have enough money to pay for a place to stay, not for both nights, it's a rocky coast.

"Like I says, I get about a hundred out there, make a pretty good piece of cash, 25 dollars sometime, more, good money back in them days, about five times what I'd make in Wortham, for sure. "See That My Grace Is Kept Clean" they all wanted that, and there'd be guitar players lined up close, tryin' to see how I worked my hands, I could feel 'em up there tryin' to listen and watch real close and I didn't like it. They'd ask to play guitar but they could never make it through a whole song and I'd say 'ain't got time to fool, boys, a man's tryin' to make a livin' out here.' But the peoples loved it and they'd come back at night, every night I'd go out there, they'd come in from the farms on the train and others walked down from up North, and they'd listen, see, it weren't like no juke joint, no dancin' crowd, they's listenin' and tappin' feet, all noddin' head, you know and that was all the dance I needed from 'em and they come back 'gain and again."

So he sang the blues and it went like this:

"Oak tree of four hundred years/ roundabout the Flood/ done by death and raintree ants and gathered up in mud.

Flowers of the hillside brood/ gabardine and lace/ decked in treble blackguard cloth and wheeled through mossy gates.

Call me on the felon tube/ shell me with a gong/ throw my wheels and bear me down/ and try me right from wrong.

Bend my way'n look real close/ terrify the seeds/ inch it out and don't come home/ the only mound that bleeds.

I'm over now my time is done/ my numbers danced the clap/ sink your wolf teeth into this/ and nevermind the crap."

And he laughed, packed up, and split!

Blind Lemon Jefferson is the King Of The Blues, and tonight he's breathin' deep in a Dallas graveyard. He ain't there to visit family, no desire to kneel and shrine coaxes this big heart. The bones beneath his feet are out of reach ot the blues, tuned to another channel, and he doesn't care, he's chasing Nellie Campbell, and she's leading him down. He's kinda drunk, swinging a bottle with his left arm. It's mad, but you can't see it in his eyes. She's workin' for her pay, that's the only way it goes off, and Mr. Lemon, he's a winner but it's never for free, Jefferson's money is his midnight friend, the only mouth that speaks up tonight, black, for a two hundred fifty pound blind guitar player, and it's the change he made, hailstones of silver, to rattle and bust the deadlock minutes, 'cause it's slow, days are long, hot and damp too and don't you wish you had an answer? Blind Lemon, least he knew the question, but now there ain't no telling.

(DE)

The Shelled Body

(for Sharon Miller)

The body gives breath
the body takes it away
the worm in the apple
light stuck in the corners of a room
fly buzz at picnic

sorrows strung like Chinese lanterns...

can you see the quivering fleck of eternity
holed up in the tumult of clouds
above the broad shimmering river
trudging towards the coal plant

in the sculpted heavy weight concrete of bridges
curvilinear and decked with metal ropes

in the half-submerged body of the frog

in the skinny-dip pond with the clumsy mosquitoes
in the knock-kneed goats in the kitchen
next to the bathroom stall covered with an old sheet

in the radon house bunked into the hillside
where farmers once treaded

can you see the quivering fleck

in the dog's fidgety tail cut off midway
in the tic that settles on one leg
eating blood for breakfast

in the waterfall trickling down
with the consistency of a good typist in 1944

in the bookstore-cum-bus stop on the main drag
in the white vinyl waterbed stuck beneath
a sky pregnant with aluminum foil stars

in the knees scraped to hell under the bridge
in the deck overlooking the transplanted trees
in the acreage sloped towards no name roads

does the body retain the fleck
as existence grinds

the body of a mortgaged life
the body once pure as sand
now the tired body
a pavilion fissured

the body as vessel
heading towards Lethe
where the body will be erased
in the mind

forever

The Season of Death Is Never Demure

(for Kathy Johnston)

this morning my heart
was full of crows
each tore at a muscle, picked tissue.
mottled clouds stirred across
highways wedged in by refineries

the grinding wheel of existence
took you during the night,
stealing heartbeats, stealing
breaths

emptiness and tumult reigned

then the sun slanted
through the wounded sky

I saw the glint of your eye
pressing forward
perfect as the corolla
of a flower

seizing the heavens.

The Bivouac of the Dead: Vicksburg, Mississippi

Never mind the tourist brochures with slanted language. Never mind
the dusty opulence of mansions next to shotgun shacks with faded
flags on desiccated tree limbs, flapping with the imprecision of
wounded butterflies.

We rounded the last green hill, pointing the car towards the cemetery
nudging the Mississippi. It was broad-shouldered, fattened, and fast,
making barges look out of control. In the summer steam, the river
offered murky miles of destruction.

Blemished white grave markers invoked terraced fields of teeth in
the amber sun. Hemmed in by kudzu -- bitter visitor from China
devouring nearby trees -- the land exuded a poetry that only the
dead, including bivouacked boys from flat Illinois prairies and
fecund Wisconsin farms, could offer.

A half-eaten, formerly mud-caked Navy gunship sat across the road,
held hostage by gawking children and dads unwilling to ungrip cell
phones.

My great-great-grandfather, shopkeeper Corwin, rose in the ranks of
the Ohio 72nd

Infantry here. Smelling his ghost, my wife and I fled mosquitoes aiming straight for our hands and faces. His enemies were buried deep in the heights of nearby Natchez, next to immigrants from Syria and Ireland.

They occupy a landscape dotted with delicate iron fences paid for by steamship captains and cotton field magnates, the capitalism that cocooned millionaires in the once unbridled South.

People still grieve there, differently. Hidden from the lonely cemetery office, ladies in minivans offer broken shells, Mardis Gras beads, small Matchbox cars and fire trucks placed on baby plots. The nearby oil derrick never stops undulating, never stops rusting.

I snap photos of chicory flavored coffee factories and Mark Twain's waterside haunt, where ferns grow out of dank walls. Hail knocks out the electrical grid in 103-degree heat. Lightning bursts in purple zigzags across the lip of nearby Louisiana.

Satellite radio, affixed to nostalgia for the days of Casio keyboards and parachute pants, emits a barrage of new wave songs.

Dinner? For those who refuse boiling crawdaddy pots, clumpy cheese-drenched pasta awaits.

Never mind the Indian mound nestled away in the itchy grass and back road bumps where tattooed teenage parents mend a broken tire; never mind the empty military school where men cheered dead Brits in New Orleans; never mind 10,100 Union men hacked to pieces by cannons while rebels hid in caves eating shoes; never mind the freed blacks driven to river camps, free to die from raids and dysentery; never mind the disappeared records stores on the blues highway; never mind the food pantries with homemade signs exclaiming "God Said, 'Though Shalt Not Steal'"; never mind the unfinished Civil Rights mural next to the stoic Southern soldier on a monolith.

Never mind the feral strands of cotton poking up from quiet Natchez Trace outside Port Gibson, with its neon cinema remnants, burger stand-cum-car wash, and collapsed buildings coughing on the edge of town.

Never mind my family swallowed by this place, never mind the bivouac, the dead.

Made in the USA
San Bernardino, CA
29 January 2015